C000186428

# Contents

# Introduction

ONE of the best-known examples of how etymology has reflected social life in Britain comes from the realm of food and cooking. In *Ivanhoe* Walter Scott portrays England in 1194 as a divided country, in which the Saxons, speaking a language in which Old English word-forms persist, are responsible for the food animals in the field, while the Normans, having no reason to alter the language they speak from that spoken by the followers of William the Conqueror, get to eat the meat. What Gurth, the swineherd, calls 'swine' and 'oxen' are called 'pork' and 'beef' by his Norman overlords. The indoor terms, deriving from Norman French, included those of cooking methods (boiling, roasting, frying) and the meats themselves (pork, mutton, veal, venison, beef). The idea of two groups of people, overlord and underdog, separated by vocabulary, was first proposed by John Wallis in 1653 in his *Grammatica Linguae Anglicanae* and can easily lead us to think of a two-tier system of language, food and English society at that time. It is partly based on a statement made in 1300 by Robert of Gloucester: 'the lower classes still stick to English and to their own language.'

However, other evidence shows a rather more complicated situation. Though French remained the language of the ruling class until about 1250, many French social customs had already been introduced into England in the reign of Edward the Confessor (1042–66) and had been eagerly taken up by the English nobility. Intermarriage between Norman and Saxon was applied as deliberate policy after the Conquest, and by the time *porc* became

# DISCOVERING WORDS IN THE KITCHEN

Julian Walker

SHIRE PUBLICATIONS

First published in Great Britain in 2010 by Shire Publications Ltd, Midland House, West Way, Botley, Oxford OX2 0PH, United Kingdom.
44-02 23rd Street, Suite 219, Long Island City, NY 11101, USA.

E-mail: shire@shirebooks.co.uk    www.shirebooks.co.uk

A CIP catalogue record for this book is available from the British Library.

Shire Discovering no. 302    •    ISBN-978 0 74780 776 6

Julian Walker has asserted his right under the Copyright, Designs and Patents Act, 1988, to be identified as the author of this book.

Designed by Tony Truscott Designs, Henfield, West Sussex, UK and typeset in Garamond.

Printed in China through Worldprint Ltd.

10  11 12  13  14    10 9 8 7 6 5 4 3 2 1

ACKNOWLEDGEMENTS
With thanks to Anne Eggebert, Fae Logie, Jonnie Robinson, Peg Tilley, and staff at the British Library. Cover photograph by Elizabeth Crawford.

DEDICATION
For Freddie and Alec.

'pork' (around 1300) the clear division between a Norman ruling class and a ruled Saxon people had disintegrated; any lexical distinction indicated that the acquisition of French vocabulary was more likely to be an activity of the rich, or those who wanted to participate in their wealth. But equally, a Norman who wanted to run anything from a manor to a country effectively had to learn to communicate with his servants and tenants, even when initially supported by a significant number of foreign mercenary soldiers. As David Burnley says in the *Cambridge History of the English Language* (2001), 'As the [twelfth] century progressed English rapidly became the first language of many Anglo-Norman families … As for native-born Englishmen, their grasp of French often appears to reflect their position, education or aspirations in the world.'

The distinction between one word for meat and another for animal arguably did exist – but in Old English, where the meat from a *cælf* was *cealfes flæsc*. Certainly the distinction between animal and meat, as in 'calf' and 'veal', returned much later; but, despite there being Old French words for 'chicken' and 'goat', there was no distinction between animal and meat in these cases, which would be expected if the separation between social groups were being maintained by word selection. If there ever was any conscious distinction, it broke down quite quickly, and Old English words to do with food and its preparation survived for centuries. The first record of *porc* for meat is dated about 1300 (*OED*), in a recognisably English text. If an animal fit for eating was being described, *porc* was used to describe a living creature well into the seventeenth century, and 'pigge-pye' is found in Hannah Wolley's *The Cook's Guide* (1664). Johnson's 1755 *Dictionary* included the use of 'beef' for a 'cow' (with the plural form 'beeves'); and as late as the early nineteenth century the word 'mutton' was used to describe a 'sheep'. An Old English word for 'boil', *sethe*, survived the entire medieval period, and a Latin/Middle English vocabulary from as late as 1425 includes under terms for meat 'swine-flesche', 'beyf-flesche', 'chepe-flesche', and so on – a mixture of Anglo-Norman and Old English words within a clearly Old English word structure.

'Cow-meat' survived in the Yorkshire dialect into the 1950s, apparently uninfluenced by nine hundred years of Anglo-Norman lexical pressure. Old English words still to be found in the kitchen are 'bake' (*bacan*), 'bowl' (*bolla*), 'pot' (*pott*), 'spoon' (*spon*, meaning 'chip') and 'kitchen' itself (*cycene*, from the Vulgar Latin *cocina*).

## How words are made

Through interaction with other languages, English has continuously adopted foreign words; 'scone' and 'juice' both come from Dutch, while the vegetable 'squash' is from Narragansett Indian. Words sometimes imitate the sound of the thing described, as for example in the dish 'bubble and squeak'. Words may arise as a result of error: 'gravy' was probably a scribe's mistaken copy of 'grany'. English has also continuously changed its own vocabulary, both in form and meaning. *Aseothan* became *sethe*, which became 'seethe', which was eventually ousted by *boille*, which became *boyle*, and later 'boil'. An Old English word for 'to die' was *steorfan*, which later developed into the form *sterven* and came to mean 'to starve' only in the sixteenth century. The Middle English word 'offal' (literally 'what falls off the table during butchering') was parallel with the originally French word 'garbage'; against the expected pattern, the French form was downgraded from 'something that could be used' to 'something to be rejected'. Cookery books until the early twentieth century offered tips on 'marketing' – the process of buying, rather than selling, in the market place.

Occasionally changes of form took place to make sense of lost derivations; known as folk etymologies, usually these were obviously erroneous and occasionally bizarre. Asparagus was for a time called 'sparrow grass', avocado pears were known as 'alligator pears', and cucumbers became 'cowcumbers'. A 'chestnut', from the Middle French *chastaigne*, has no connection with chests and is not a nut. Sometimes all sense was lost, often when foreign words were anglicised: 'quelque-choses' became 'kickshaws', nasturtium flowers became 'astertion flowers', and in Indian English champagne became 'simpkin'. Occasionally a simple, apparently rational change of spelling produced a word patently at odds with the evidence: crayfish are not fish, and walnuts, spelt *wallnuts* for some time, do not grow on or near walls.

## Foods from abroad

Food is one of the great fields of interaction between peoples, sometimes positively, sometimes negatively: colonial administrators and soldiers, returning home, have usually brought back the tastes and foodstuffs of the people they set out to rule, while for centuries the French and English have taunted each other as 'frog-eaters' or 'rosbifs'. As other cultures have influenced social life in England, and later Britain, the introduction of tastes, foods and methods have all left their mark on the English language.

That the Romans found the diet offered in first-century Britain inadequate can be seen from the foods they imported: many herbs, garlic, onions, parsnips, peas, turnips, celery, lettuce, cucumber and leeks, and the curious fermented fish-paste essential to the Roman palate, known as *liquamen*. Spices such as ginger and cinnamon were imported from the other side of the world (the spice route to China was established by the second century), and peacock, pheasants, rabbits and snails were introduced. Though the Romans never ceased to import *liquamen* from Mediterranean producers, there was a flow in the other direction, as Colchester oysters were sent to Rome, along with cereal products.

Around the time of Claudius' invasion of Britain the oldest European cookery book was compiled by Apicius. Called *De Re Coquinaria*, its first word is quite familiar – *recipe*, the Latin for 'take' (though the first line is less likely to feature in a contemporary kitchen – 'Take and pluck the flamingo'). However, the earliest Latin in English speech arrived via the Germanic languages, which had been absorbing it for six hundred years.

It is difficult to tell how much of Roman culinary culture survived the departure of the legions at the beginning of the fifth century; some Roman introductions such as walnuts seem to have become dormant, while rabbits (improbably) disappeared until they were reintroduced by the Normans, and others were probably reintroduced by Christian missionaries as medicine rather than food. This was the case with spices and herbs particularly. Trade along the spice routes survived the end of the Roman Empire, and in 735 the Anglo-Saxon historian Bede bequeathed to his fellow monks prunes, raisins, lavender, aniseed, cinnamon, cloves, cubebs, cumin, coriander, cardamom, ginger, sugar and pepper.

Some of the arrivals during this period are startling: figs and olive oil were imported, peaches and grapes were grown, and lettuces were reintroduced. In a community where what people ate was in large measure governed by the Church, fish and seafood figured largely in the diet; this ranged from whales to cockles, pike to minnows. As the major economic resource, food was governed by rules: individual estates such as Glastonbury Abbey had their own statutes as to who was entitled to what from the slaughtering of animals; horse meat was forbidden by the Church (a prohibition which has lasted, except for a period in the nineteenth century), and food that fell to the floor was consigned to the Devil.

Anglo-Saxon cooking combined tastes from a wide range of sources – cranes, porpoises, gulls' eggs and thistles, foods that are no longer deemed appropriate by modern sensibilities or marketing strategies. Many of their words for foods are still with us (broth, cheese, salt), but the waves of Scandinavian settlement brought many words into Old English, in some cases supplanting the existing word; eventually the Old Norse *egg* supplanted *ey*, and the spelling of 'kettle' with *k* prevailed.

## The Middle Ages

The influence of French culture on English developed during the eleventh century, accelerating after 1066. The new social structure with established centres of power, particularly stone castles, meant that after the initial period of conflict and devastation the status of cooking rose; twenty years after Hastings two royal cooks were holding manorial rights. From this period we have most of the words for different types of cooking, as well as names for the cuts of meat, and the words for many kinds of recipe, such as liquor, pie and sauce. The incorporation of Anglo-Norman into Middle English was slow and inconsistent, as outlined above. A mid-thirteenth-century vocabulary shows the process happening, sometimes the French term ousting the English, sometimes vice versa: Latin *porius* (leek) was translated as *poret* and *lek*; Latin *lactuca* (lettuce) was translated as *letue* and *slep-wurt*. Some Anglo-Norman terms were lost, to reappear as part of the later Latin revival: Alexander Neckam, writing in about 1180, used the words *escuele* and *quele* for a 'bowl' or 'dish', which reappeared much later as 'esculent'. Other Anglo-Norman words, such as *henap* for a 'bowl' or 'cup', became obsolete and were eventually revived only as antiquarian terms.

After 1250 returning Crusaders brought with them recipes and ingredients from the eastern Mediterranean and beyond, including sugar ('honey-reed'), mace and nutmeg (an alteration of *noix muscade*, Old French for 'nut smelling of musk'); Arabic influence on English cooking grew with the introduction of almonds, raisin paste and rose-water. During the fourteenth century the visual aspect of food became more important, and spices such as sandalwood and saffron were used for colour as much as taste. The range of the cost of ingredients increased as grocers made fortunes by importing luxuries: in 1300 a pound of sugar, now a food ingredient rather than a medicine, cost the equivalent of eight dozen eggs. 'Sumptuary' laws in the fourteenth century limited what and how much could be eaten by people at various levels of society.

Glossaries of the period show Middle English words that are fairly recognisable, with the surviving pre-Conquest vocabulary mixing with Anglo-Norman terms to give words such as *crok-styke* (literally 'pot stick', from Old English *crocc*, meaning 'pot', giving modern 'crockery'), or *frynn-panne* ('frying pan', from Old French *frire*, meaning 'to fry', and Old English *panne* or *ponne*, meaning 'pan').

Peasant food had remained much the same for a thousand years – bread and ale, with root vegetables (*worts*, or 'pot-herbs' if the leaves were being eaten), broth, frumenty (boiled wheat), pease (ground legumes) and occasionally meat. Often, however, the poor would taste the spices of the wealthy. In rich households, sauce-based food was poured on to bread (a trencher), there being a strict hierarchy of the kind of bread according to the status of the person; at the end of the meal, the sauce-sodden bread was given to beggars at the door of the household. Merchants, clerics and guild members might eat *roste gose* (7d in 1378), *capoun*, *pococke* or *conye*, depending on their circumstances.

The *Forme of Cury* (about 1390) is the earliest surviving English cookery book, giving an insight into both cookery and language at a period of transition. At Henry IV's marriage feast in 1399 the menu was in a mixture of Middle English and French. It included 'Crustarde Lumbarde', a pie of cream, eggs, dates, sugar and prunes; 'Gely', made from calf's foot with wine and vinegar; 'Quyncys in Comfite', quinces in syrup; and 'Eyroun engele', eggs in jelly. Within a hundred years the first English printer, William Caxton, would decide that the southern word *eyroun* would be replaced by the northern word 'eggs', and a century later a 'crustarde' had lost both its first 'r' and its piecrust. The range of sea and river creatures eaten by the wealthy included swordfish, porpoise, lobsters and sturgeon, despite the tradition that labelled sturgeon and whale as 'royal fish', dating back to Saxon times but formalised in a statute of Edward II in 1317. Archbishop Neville's coronation feast in York in 1466, in which scarcely credible amounts of food were consumed (204 cranes for example, and 25,000 gallons of wine) did not include sturgeon; but guests were served lampreys (a curious eel-like fish), a surfeit of which had famously despatched Henry I in 1135 (the phrase written by Robert Fabyan in about 1513 was originally 'a surfet by etynge of a lamprey', a 'surfeit' being in this case a medical condition brought about by overeating).

Many medieval recipes were based on Roman ideas, expressed in Latin or French – particularly important in this was the Galenic theory of humours applied to food. According to this system, which survived well into the eighteenth century, an individual's predisposition to a particular 'humour' could be balanced by eating the right sort of food, cooked in the right way. The humours were: sanguine, warm and moist, from the blood; choleric, warm and dry, from the yellow bile; phlegmatic, cold and moist, from the phlegm; and melancholic, cold and dry, from the black bile. Thus beef (moist) could be roasted to make it dry, to balance the temper of someone thought to be phlegmatic; Evelyn in 1709 was still discussing the merits of hyssop to treat melancholy, or mustard 'to dissipate Phlegmatick Humours'.

The fifteenth century saw the beginning of sugar cultivation within Europe, leading to a drop in price. This led to wider use, possibly overuse; the wealthy enjoyed increasingly inventive desserts (*subtleties* were sculptural devices of sugar and almond paste), partly as a display of wealth, but at the same time there was a growing interest in salty dishes. Whereas previously pies had largely been a way of holding meats for baking or preserving, the invention of shortcrust pastry led to pies being made to be eaten; this, with the Italian discovery that egg-whites could clarify jellies, brought the possibility of more exciting designs for dishes, with heraldic, architectural and fanciful constructions appearing on the dinner tables of the rich.

## *The Tudors and Stuarts*

The Tudor period saw many changes, among them the increasing use of milk, cream and butter, the introduction of new foods from the New World, and the awareness of different national styles of cooking. In 1520 at the Field of Cloth of Gold, the King of France 'had his meat dressed after the French fashion, and the King of England had the like after the English fashion'. In 1577 William Harrison complained that the nobility of England were employing cooks who were 'for the most part Frenchmen and strangers'. Certainly far more food was being introduced and imported into the country, with names that became gradually anglicised – potatoes, cardoons, oranges (sometimes called 'pottongayles' at this time).

Some of the words in use then have developed, while others have disappeared or become limited to regional or dialect use: *raysons of Coraunce* (Corinth) have become 'currants', *sallet* has become 'salad', and *bisket* is now 'biscuit', but *skirret*, a root vegetable, is no longer in use, and *collop*, 'a slice of meat', is used in Scotland but seldom elsewhere. As gardening became an opportunity for displays of wealth and ingenuity, the range of vegetables available for the table increased. Pickling developed, as well as candying flowers and fruits in sugar, widening the range of foods preserved for use in winter. Tudor cuisine linked the medieval world and the modern; recipes like *mawmenny* (minced chicken and pork poached with wine and flavoured with spices including cloves and fried almonds) recall dishes from an earlier age, while the custom of finishing a meal with a salad could come from a current diet.

Early-seventeenth-century changes included the use of the word 'pudding' to include both a 'sausage' and a mixture of ingredients in a bag, boiled or steamed. Potatoes appeared in recipes, and salads were boiled. Among the new foods and words were 'bonanas', 'maccaroni', 'yoghurd', 'colieflorie', and later broccoli, tea and coffee. *Farces*, meat and other ingredients shredded and stuffed into joints, poultry or bread, continued a medieval practice of pulverising meats, while the *New Booke of Cookerie* (1615), gave recipes for cooking 'sparrowes', 'larkes', 'woodcockes' and 'black-birdes', and a pie for a 'curlew or hearnshoe' – 'Put them in deepe Coffins [pie-cases], with store of Butter, and let the heads hang out for a show.' In *Country Contentments or the English Housewife* (1623) Gervase Markham's recipe for 'Olepotridge', which would develop into 'hotchpotch', seemed to contain anything available, including a leg of beef, half a pig, venison, small birds, marigold leaves and flowers.

This abundance ended with Cromwell's Commonwealth. The Puritans forbade the use of spices and sugar in cooking, but even so there were new foods – 'pistachioes', 'capers', 'fricaces' and 'anchoves' (from the Spanish, Portuguese and Basque *anchoas*). Vegetables, traditionally food for the poor, made up much of the diet, even for the aristocracy, except that they were still not called 'vegetables', but 'roots and herbs'. A 1656 text by William Coles encouraged people to eat asparagus, alexanders, elder, nettle tops, comfrey, the roots of tulips, and the tops of hops and turnips.

As if released from restriction, at the Restoration of the monarchy in 1660 recipes blossomed. In *The Closet* (1669) Kenelme Digbie introduced what became the traditional English breakfast of bacon and eggs, gave a recipe for a cake that incorporated thirty eggs, a pound of sugar, a pint and a half of cream, and nearly five pounds of butter; and he used 'ambergrease' and musk in a recipe for black pudding. Innovation and science were applied to cooking, with Papin's 1682 'digestorie', a pressure cooker, allowing the quick processing of bones for jelly and thickening. But also to be found were what may be considered unethical food: Digbie's instructions for 'cram'd chicken' involved overfeeding chickens till they could not stand. Cod was becoming fashionable, but fish mostly was taking second place to meat, despite the popularity of Izaak Walton's *Compleat Angler* (1652), with its recipe for minnow-tansy (omelette). 'Brandewine' (brandy), 'champaigne' and 'Spanish chaculate' appeared after the Restoration, and the 'sillabub' acquired its dramatic reputation. Limes and 'shaddocks' (grapefruit) appeared and in 1668 John Evelyn tasted a 'pine apple' while dining with the King. But in *A Journey to London* (1698) Samuel Sorbière remarked on the almost total absence of leaf vegetables in most Londoners' diets, 'grey-pease', meat and bread being the food of the 'common people', while the well-off had vegetables 'well pepper'd and salted, and swimming in butter'.

The awareness of cooking as an expression of national identity can be seen in the conscious retention of French and Italian names – Markham in 1623 rendered as *Quelquechoses* a recipe that had appeared in 1615 as 'Kicks Hawes', and Digbie in 1669 kept the Italian *pancotto* and the French *champignons*. Samuel Pepys took his wife to dine at 'a French House' (restaurant) in 1661, and by the end of the century French influence extended to menus and table layouts. The reputations and recipes of La Varenne and Massialot meant that

French cooking could be used as a display of status, provoking a middle-class reaction in which English recipes became 'plain cooking' – Evelyn's 'solid meat' and Rochester's 'our own plain fare'.

## Georgian and Victorian Britain

The almost frenetic energy with which eighteenth-century people approached food is exemplified in Dr Johnson, who ate with such vigour that the veins on his head stood out and he poured with sweat. The wealthy took to eating away from home and an interest in food became a mark of taste. Improvements in agriculture meant that there was more food around: by 1750 cattle had doubled in size since the medieval period. As the amount of beef available grew, it became a national symbol, 'the roast beef of Old England', as in Hogarth's 1748 painting. Clearly much of this was aimed at France, explicitly in the case of Hannah Glasse, whose *Art of Cookery made Plain and Easy* (1747) blasted those who 'would rather be impos'd on by a French Booby, than give encouragement to a good English cook'. It is in Glasse's book that we find the first use of the word *monsieur* for the green fat used to make turtle soup. Later in the century people were unimpressed by the French aspect of the cooking in the newly rediscovered *Forme of Cury*.

There were still links to the past – Glasse includes recipes for lampreys; but she also was aware of foreign foods from far away, so that elder shoots are used in imitation of bamboo. Recipes appear excessive to modern eyes – Farley in *The London Art of Cookery* (1783) gives a recipe for a cake with thirty-six eggs, and one for roast rabbits, boned, with their flesh minced and then stuck back over their skeletons (with bones placed to give them 'horns'); while Bailey's *Household Dictionary* (1736) gives a recipe for 'barbitued kid', boned, roast, quartered, boiled, baked and reconstructed, with marrow, 'pistachoes', veal, champagne, shallots and watercress. This was the period when it was felt that cruelty at the point of slaughter would make meat more tender. Small wonder that towards the end of the century more people began to realise the value of vegetables, especially the potato.

During this period fewer words were adopted from the Continent than arrived as a result of Britain's foreign trade, colonial expansion and the business of exploration: 'meringue' and 'semolina' show continuing adoptions from French and Italian, but 'chutney' (Hindi), 'chowder' (Canadian French), 'piccalilli' (Indonesia), 'yam' (West Africa via Portuguese), 'vodka' (Russian) and 'barbecue' (Haiti via Spanish) between them take us most of the way round the world.

As the century progressed, the Industrial Revolution took people away from unadventurous but generally available fresh food, and an increasing number of city dwellers were forced to survive on watery soups devoid of nutrition, cheese with adulterated bread, tea, sugar and bacon. The poor were offered maize and rice, but often without instructions on how to cook them. As the cost of food rose in the nineteenth century, 'soup-kitchens' appeared (1839); measures to alleviate hunger included the reintroduction of 'poullenta' (polenta) in Alexis Soyer's *Charitable Cookery or the Poor Man's Regenerator* (1847).

During the nineteenth century the American national identity became entrenched in the language by Webster's management and direction of spelling in his *American Dictionary of the English Language* (1828), including words such as 'omelet', 'flavor' and 'pompion'; 'cooky' (from Scotland, and now more often 'cookie') appeared in Worcester's *Universal and Critical Dictionary*, published in Boston in 1850.

Maria Rundell's *Domestic Happiness*, published in 1809, contained the first recipes for 'tomata sauce' and sold half a million copies in twenty years, yet, according to William Cobbett, 'to buy the thing ready-made is the taste of the day'. Following the French Revolution, exiled cooks of the calibre of Carême reintroduced French cuisine to England, a taste that was reinforced by the cheap gourmandising available in Paris after the Napoleonic Wars. This was continued by Soyer, whose first book was called *The Gastronomic Regenerator* (1846), and is seen in Isabella Beeton's mixed French and English ('lobster curry en casserole') in the menus in her *Household Management* (1861). French cuisine did not have a monopoly on taste; Italian ices were enormously fashionable at all levels of society, and the first Indian and Chinese restaurants in London were opened before the First World War.

At the beginning of the nineteenth century meat was tenderised by being hung till it was nearly uneatable, and vegetables were still secondary to meat; Kitchiner's *The Cook's Oracle* (1823) recommended that boiled salad was 'far more wholesome than the Raw Salad', and omitted 'lettuce' and 'salad' from its index. The industrial, commercial and agricultural revolutions combined to change the nature of supplied food. Railways delivered fresh produce to the cities; refrigerated ships brought cheap meat from the far side of the world; canning and bottling preserved food longer, and with better taste, than the centuries-old techniques of salting, smoking and fermenting. Colman, Crosse & Blackwell, Lea & Perrins, Cadbury, Peak Frean and others created foods that did half the cook's job, and the 'cooker' was available from 1884, along with a battery of kitchen tools which to the uninitiated were simply 'gadgets' (1886).

Not everyone shared in the abundance: children were often deliberately underfed as this was held to promote stronger characters; the poor were advised to make puddings from suet, water, salt and flour as this would fill their stomachs, and many were content to eat 'leftovers', first found in 1891 (*OED*), though recipes using left-over food had been available since the 1760s. In reaction to Mrs Beeton's four-course meals with up to twenty-four dishes, including eight different kinds of meat, the first 'health-food' shop was opened in 1898, selling American breakfast 'cereals' (1899). The first use of the word 'vegetarian' is dated to 1839 (*OED*), though Martha Brotherton's *Vegetable Cooking* was published in 1812.

## *The twentieth century*

By 1914 Britain was largely dependent on imported food so that, when war broke out and food shortages became desperate, cookery writers had recourse to old food names as a way of giving a desirable gloss to unappetising dishes: thin brown soup became 'crowdie', and boiled rabbit was served as 'galantine'. As in the post-Commonwealth seventeenth century, post-war Britain opened itself both to foreign food influences and the possibility of a wider range of home-grown foods. The banana, the grapefruit and the 'cantaloupe' melon (named after a Vatican estate where the fruit was introduced from Armenia) became familiar; salads suited diets to fit the new thin fashions, and recipes such as Chicken Maryland and the Waldorf salad began a stream of influence from the United States that has continued to the present. From 1920 the 'fridge' was seen in a growing number of British kitchens, and 'hors d'oeuvre' (French for 'out of the ordinary') became a regular dish. The growth of cookery writing provided scope for cookery to develop its own language, from 'fold', as in 'folding eggs into a mixture' (1915), to 'drizzle', as in 'to drizzle honey over a joint', (1950s).

Rationing and food shortages in the Second World War brought a grim ingenuity and the arrival of institutional Orwellian language: the 'National Loaf' was legally adulterated with chalk to help calcium intake, and vegetable-filled 'Woolton Pie', named after the Minister of Food but invented by a chef at the Savoy Hotel, outraged the sensibilities of those brought up on meat, vegetables and gravy. The middle of the twentieth century saw few introductions of new words into the field of food and cooking; rationing and shortages brought a familiarity with 'Spam' (an invented name, not a shortening of 'spiced ham') and 'snoek' (a South African tinned sea-fish, though the word is Dutch for 'pike'). British food in the post-war era had a reputation for dullness, which may have had the effect of making people more ready to be influenced by foreign food, whether the American convenience foods such as 'pizza' (ultimately from a late Latin word for 'flat bread'), or French, Italian, Greek or Spanish cuisine. Eventually this would lead to familiarity with such food words as *sushi* (a Japanese word known since the late nineteenth century), *tapas*

(Spanish for 'covers', referring to the portions of food being of a size to cover a wine-glass) and *meze* (Greek for 'snack', deriving ultimately from the Persian *mazidan*, meaning 'to taste').

The 1960s and 1970s saw meals characterised by bottled sauces, tasteless sliced white bread and tinned spaghetti, as well as a returning awareness of robust British recipes, such as pies, beef olives and herb omelettes. Television chefs gave a sudden familiarity to 'couscous' (via French, from the Arabic for 'to pound into small amounts'), 'filo pastry', 'bulgar', 'okra' and 'tamarind' (from the Arabic *tamr-hindi*, meaning 'Indian date'), but also revived old-fashioned local ingredients such as fennel (Old English *finul*) and rhubarb.

In the 1980s, as food became fashionable, *nouvelle cuisine* was followed by an influx of foreign foods encountered through increased foreign travel. New foods appeared: *ciabatta*, an Italian bread designed to compete with the French baguette (*ciabatta* means 'an old shoe'); *quorn*, a fungus-based meat alternative, named after Quorndon, a village near the first production centre; *balti*, a kind of curry originally popular in Birmingham, taking its name from its pot, and traditionally eaten with bread direct from the pan; and *chicken tikka masala* (Hindi 'small marinaded pieces of meat' with Urdu 'spices'), developed as a British variation on an Indian theme. As cookery became television entertainment, the vocabulary used grew more excitable: Gordon Ramsay employs liberal amounts of the Old English vocabulary that had been displaced by post-Norman sensibilities; trifle sponges are 'wodged' into the base of a glass bowl in Nigella Lawson's recipe for Anglo-Italian trifle, while Jamie Oliver's website offers 'recipease'.

## *The names of meals*

In some cases the relationships between words are clouded by combinations of influencing factors involving age, social class and regional variation. Here it makes sense to treat words in groups: each of 'lunch', 'dinner', 'tea' and 'supper' have changed their timings and substance as the others have risen or fallen in significance.

As regards 'lunch', 'dinner', 'tea' and 'supper', the historical relationship between dinner and supper is clearest. Dinner has gradually moved later through the day: William the Conqueror dined at 9 a.m., Henry VII dined at 11 a.m., Pepys in 1667 dined at 1 p.m. and ate supper before going to bed; by 1780 dinner was eaten between 3 and 5 p.m. and now it is not uncommon to have dinner at 9 p.m. Palmer, in *Movable Feasts* (1952), gave a model of 'dinner at 1, supper at 8; luncheon at 1, dinner at 8' drawn from nineteenth-century mealtime habits and names; it indicates the central role of dinner, echoing De Quincy's early-Victorian four rules for dinner (the principal meal of the day, the meal of hospitality, a meal centred on animal food, the one which would prevail if all the rest were abandoned). Now people more often eat 'lunch' and 'supper', reserving 'dinner' for formal occasions; *The Oxford Guide to British and American Culture* (2000) states that 'dinner sounds more formal than supper – invitations are to dinner rather than supper.' Fish and chips bought at a takeaway in Scotland is, as we would expect, a 'fish supper' rather than a 'fish dinner', but meals eaten in front of the television are usually 'TV dinners' rather than 'TV suppers'. In Canada the two words are used interchangeably, while 'dinner' is more common in the United States.

'Dinner' as the midday meal remains general usage in the North of England and Scotland. Palmer points out that 'lunch' is a time as much as a meal, and the same may be said of 'dinnertime'. 'School dinners' are not limited to the Midlands and further north, though 'school lunches' are making inroads.

There is a long history of class distinction in meals, even to the point of legislation in the medieval period over who could eat what, how much and when. Kate Fox in *Watching the English* (2004) proposes that there are clear social class differences between those who use 'dinner' or 'supper' for an ordinary meal eaten at 7 p.m., and between those who call midday meals 'lunch' or 'dinner'; *The Oxford Guide to British and American Culture* states that 'in Britain the word *dinner* is used differently according to a person's social class or the place they come from'. But the distinctions by class, age and region overlap – children anywhere may be more likely to use 'dinner' than 'lunch', and 'tea' rather than 'dinner', while subjective perceptions and the social and geographical movement of people confuse the lexical pattern of a society where class is variously seen as irrelevant, avoidable, persistent or pernicious.

'Tea' is also used widely in many parts of Britain and Ireland, for adults, families, and particularly for the evening meal for children, leaving us with at least three distinct meanings: a main evening family meal, a children's early evening meal and 'tea, sandwiches and cakes'. In the United States 'afternoon tea' is rare and very posh, almost an antiquated memory of leisured courtesy visits in the eighteenth century, when the habit started; a *Delineator* booklet of 1931, published in New York, tries to put the reader at her ease – 'Afternoon tea is such an informal affair' – probably not very successfully. 'High tea' is defined by the *OED* as 'a tea at which meat is served', but the first example given, from 1831, places the meal at nine in the evening. Probably the only sure definition of 'supper' is that, like Pepys's supper, it is the last meal of the day, usually carrying implications of being lighter the later it is eaten.

Similar movements and distinctions exist for 'sweet', 'dessert', 'afters' and 'pudding'. 'Afters', now seldom heard but widely used during the Second World War and afterwards especially by children, was originally military slang, documented by Partridge from 1909. 'Pudding' is less formal than 'dessert' or 'sweet', a spoken rather than written word, the origin of its usage lying in the sweet puddings of the eighteenth century. Under the terms of Alan Ross's and Nancy Mitford's social classification of words into 'U' and 'non-U', 'pudding' was infinitely preferable to 'sweet'.

'Dessert' came into use about 1600, the French word for the fruit and jellies served after the main course was taken away (from the Latin *dis-servire*), and eventually replacing the 'banquet' in the eighteenth century. It has been more widely used in the United States and Canada, where it does not carry any class connotations; in Britain it has retained some of the foreignness which originally made it a fashionable word. In the topsy-turvy world of lexical social anthropology, 'dessert' now may be seen equally as *arriviste* or neutral, while 'pudding', formerly identifiable as northern usage, is used by more or less anyone. Lady Jekyll's *Kitchen Essays* (1930) give recipes for 'sweets' and, less often, 'desserts' for 'the pudding course': thus in Britain one could have a sweet for pudding, while in the United States the same thing could be a pudding for dessert.

## *International variations*

The marketing in recent years of 'kettle chips' in Britain is a fair indicator of how words develop separately in different areas, and also of how contact between areas leads to cross-fertilisation. The appeal and familiarity of some American products mean that only a pedantic British English-speaker would assume that 'kettle chips' are French fried potatoes cooked in a vessel with a spout used exclusively for boiling water. But a reader of *Chambers's Etymological Dictionary* in 1867 would not have found these definitions for 'chip' or 'kettle' either.

It is not only between Britain and the United States that different usages or vocabulary are found; these are likely to occur wherever English is spoken. In the United States a 'kettle' is a wide vessel for boiling liquids in – for boiling water for a teapot, when such a vessel is required, the term 'tea-kettle' is used. In Canada and Australia a 'kettle' is the same as in Britain; in South Africa a 'kettle' is a still. In the United States and Australia a 'crumpet' is as in the Britain, but a 'muffin' (in the Britain and Canada a thick round savoury cake), from the German *muffe*, meaning 'small cake', is a light sweet cake containing chocolate or fruits. In the United States 'ketchup' or 'catsup' is used where British or Canadian English has 'ketchup', while in the United States and Canada 'candy' covers what Australians and British call 'sweets'. A 'lollipop' in Canada and Britain is either a sugary sweet on a stick or a frozen confection on a stick ('ice-lolly'), while in the United States and Australia this would be a boiled sweet on a stick only; in the United States, and occasionally in Canada, a frozen confection on a stick would be called a 'popsicle'. In India 'a toast' is equivalent to 'a piece of toast' in Britain, and tea without milk is called 'black tea', as in Australia.

In Britain the main difference between 'shrimp' and 'prawn' is one of size, though some supermarkets sell shrimps as 'small prawns' on the assumption that greater size will be read as better taste, or more likely slightly socially exclusive (and therefore more expensive). In the United States the term 'prawn' has almost disappeared; American 'shrimp' (the plural usually without 's') come in all sizes, including 'jumbo shrimp', though on the west coast larger ones may be called 'prawns'. In Australia 'prawn' is used for most sizes, though a television tourist advertising campaign mainly directed at the United States invented the expression 'put another shrimp on the barbie'.

## Lost words and forgotten dishes

As well as gaining words from other languages, English has lost words, and once familiar dishes have vanished with their names.

Among the words that have been lost are *broil* (to grill, retained in America and being reintroduced to Britain), *farce* (to stuff), *manchet* (a small loaf), *cullis* (a broth), *ramayle* (scrapings), *mango* (to pickle), *skirret* (a woody carrot) and *smoore* (to brown meat). Perhaps few would mourn the rarity of 'tapioca' and 'sago' ('fish eyes' to a generation of children), *pottage* ('anything boiled or decocted for food', Johnson, 1755, effectively now 'casserole') or soup thickened with bread or cereal, or *frumenty* or *furmity*, a dish of husked wheat with milk, eggs and sugar. Few now would dare to cook a pike, a lamprey or a cow's udder, formerly favoured dishes; and unfavourable sound associations do not help the cause of *sops* (milk and egg-yolks poured over bread), *sewe* (a broth) and *junket* (milk set with rennet).

Now lost or very rare foods that were once popular include 'quince jelly', a Tudor favourite; *orache* ('It is a never to be omitted ingredient of our sallets,' said Evelyn in 1706); the *posset*, a warm comforting drink of hot cream, wine or beer, whipped eggs and spices; *jursylle* or *jussell* (eggs and grated bread, boiled in broth and seasoned with sage and saffron); though *jumballs* (eighteenth-century biscuits made of almonds, cream and flour) survived as 'Jumble: Kind of sweet, sticky cake' (in Wyld's *Universal Dictionary of the English Language*, 1936), and as a name for sweets in the East Midlands into the 1950s.

Spices and herbs in use a thousand years ago but now ignored include 'cubebs', a spice used from Anglo-Saxon times instead of pepper; 'galingale', aromatic root spice; and tansy, which gave its name to the omelette. Though the names may be different, Christmas food includes 'verjuice', the pulp of a sour fruit to accompany meat, and 'hippocras', red wine sweetened and spiced (so called because it was strained in sleeves like those of the legendary physician Hippocrates). Other sweet wines were malmsey, from Cyprus, and metheglin, a kind of mead. We might not now see the appeal of *porray* (mashed leeks) or *flummery* (cold boiled wheat with cream or alcohol), and *mawmenny* (ground chicken in spiced sauce) has an unappealing name; but *galantine* (cold fowl in sauce or jelly) and *succade* (candied peel) could be modern brand-names.

## *Modern times*

As marketing has made us more aware of brands, there has been increasing protection of names to preserve local production. Whisky may be made in Japan, and camembert in Germany, but champagne can now only be made in Champagne, and Stilton in three English counties. This may seem restrictive and against the spirit of change that keeps language alive, but at least it may guard against the labelling of absurdities such as Margaret Dods's 1826 'gooseberry champagne' (in *The Cook and Housewife's Manual*). Legislation and common sense do not always march side by side: in 2004 the European Union declared that carrots were fruit, and in 2009 a legal ruling decided that though Pringles contained only 42 per cent potato they were a potato snack rather than a cake, thus landing their makers with a hefty tax bill.

The late twentieth century brought an influx of new words into the kitchen as the expansion of holiday destinations brought people into contact with Thai, Tex-Mex, Japanese and other cuisines. Some of these words moved across directly, some were anglicised, and some indicated a dismantling of barriers and attitudes that brought an almost childlike abandonment of any rules of cooking (what other explanation could there be for deep-fried Mars bars?). The development of cookery as enjoyable and creative led to the wider use of more expressive phrases, such as 'to wilt spinach' or 'to drizzle sauce'. The creation of new words for foods such as the self-explanatory 'banoffee pie' or the creation of terms for carving meat in the late medieval period show that the development of cooking and vocabulary have always gone hand in hand.

## *A note on languages and their periods*

The Germanic group of languages, to which English belongs, is a branch of the Indo-European language family. I have used the term 'Latin' to mean Classical Latin, known from written texts made during the Roman Republic and Empire. 'Greek' refers to the Greek used in the last five hundred years BC.

The peoples who migrated from the Continent to England from around AD 450 spoke a range of West Germanic dialects. They migrated initially from the Danish peninsula and the coastal areas to the south-west as far as the mouth of the Rhine.

Old English developed in different dialects throughout England, though early written texts are surprisingly similar, deriving mostly from the West Saxon area; after the Norman Conquest it was the dialect of the East Midlands and London that became the antecedent of standard English.

Old Frisian, from about 700 to 1500, was spoken along the coastline between the Rhine and the Elbe; Old Saxon was spoken up to about 1000 along coastal areas of northern Germany.

Languages in Europe developed while Middle English was developing in England. Middle Low German was spoken in the northern Germanic area (based around the North Sea and the

Baltic Sea) from about 1100 to 1600. Middle Dutch was used to the west and Middle High German to the south from about 1100 to 1600. Old Norse was spoken in the Scandinavian countries from about 800 to 1300. The westward migration of the Franks from Germany from the third century influenced the Latin spoken in northern France that they adopted, classed as Late Latin. This developed divergent forms in speech (Vulgar Latin) and writing (Medieval Latin); Vulgar Latin evolved into Old French around the ninth century. Medieval Latin continued to be used in Europe through the medieval period.

Norman French was French spoken in Normandy, as opposed to Parisian French, spoken in northern France outside Normandy and Brittany during the medieval period; it was influenced by the Vikings who settled in Normandy. This was the language spoken by the Normans in England from 1066, but it developed mixed forms in Anglo-Norman. Anglo-Norman (sometimes called Anglo-French) was French spoken in England after 1066, which was influenced over time by Parisian French. Middle French is considered to have lasted from about 1300 to 1600.

The Old English letter *æ*, which I have retained, was pronounced as a short vowel; the letter *þ* (unvoiced *th*) I have written as *th*; and *ð* (voiced *th*) I have written as *th*.

# Fruit

**Apple**. The apple is perhaps the archetypal fruit, signifying not merely 'an apple' but the concept of fruit in general, and serving as a basis for building the identity of other fruits and vegetables (tomatoes and potatoes have names in other languages that stem from or include the word for 'apple', and both cucumbers and, bizarrely, mandragora were 'earth apples' in Old English). Though there is the possibility of a Latin pun in Genesis (*malum* may mean 'bad' or 'apple'), the Vulgate, the fourth-century translation of the Bible into Latin, follows Hebrew in using a word that means nothing more specific than 'fruit'. By the seventh century the word in use in England was *æppel*, but this was used to signify any fruit or vegetable until well into the Middle English period, which may explain the confusion (but see **banana**). *Æppel* was possibly an early acquisition from Latin – perhaps from the name of the southern Italian town of Abella, described by Virgil as *malifera*, meaning 'bearer of apples'. This may sound far-fetched, but 'pearmain' apples, now rare, derived via Old French *permain* from the Latin *parmensis*, meaning 'from Parma'. A fifteenth-century vocabulary translates the Latin *pomum* as *a nappylle*, but, as it gives *nonyon* for 'onion' and *nospytalle* for 'hospital', the scribe may just have had trouble placing the 'n' of the indefinite article.

Modern varieties of apple mostly bear the names of those who cultivated them. Bramley apples had been in use for at least forty years before being recognised as a new variety in the 1850s – the original tree was in the Nottinghamshire garden of Matthew Bramley. In the 1830s Cox's Orange Pippins were first grown by Richard Cox in Slough, and the Granny Smith was first grown by Maria Ann Smith, who emigrated from Sussex to Australia in 1838; her sons-in-law named the variety after her, though it is not documented until 1895 (*OED*). Golden Delicious were first marketed in West Virginia in 1914 following a chance find in an orchard of a tree bearing a hybridised fruit of unknown parentage.

Hannah Glasse (1747) has an appendix on marketing (at that time the business of getting the best deals at market) with monthly recommendations for fruits available. The January section contains the following apples: John apples, Winter Queenings, Marygold and Harvey, Pom-water, Golden-dorset, Renneting, Love's Pearmain and Winter Pearmain.

Other old varieties include the *codling*, formerly *quodling* and *querdling*, from the Old English *quert*, meaning 'hard', so 'fit to keep'. Having no connection with the custard apple, the 'costard', a variety that had pronounced ribs (*costes* in Anglo-Norman) on the outside, was common from the fourteenth century to the seventeenth and gave its name to 'costermongers', who were originally apple sellers.

**Apricot**. Smythe Palmer (1882) points out that *apricot* was adopted by Arabic from Latin, before being returned to the Romance languages. The Arabic article *al* was added to the Latin *praecoqua*, meaning 'early ripe' (or 'precocious'), becoming *al-barqûq*, which developed into the French *abricot* and the Portuguese *albricoque*. In the sixteenth century these provided two English forms, 'abricock' and 'abricoct', the second developing into 'apricot'; by 1750 the two forms were in use, but Webster in 1828 gave only 'apricot'.

**Banana**. In a south Asian version of the creation myth, in which Eden was situated in Sri Lanka, the Tree of Knowledge was the banana tree, which supplied both the fruit and the leaves that featured in the story of Adam and Eve. This is reflected in early

European names: *figue du paradis* or *figue d'Adam* in French, *fico d'Adamo* in Italian, and 'Adam's fig' in English. These terms were in use simultaneously with variations of *musa*, which appeared in sixteenth- and early-seventeenth-century English as 'mauz' or 'muse'; an early appearance of the word in English (1597, *OED*) explicitly links bananas to 'the Muses of Egypt and Soria'. Linnaeus reportedly adopted 'muse' in setting the scientific name for the banana genus, *Musa*, referring to Antonius Musa, physician to the Emperor Augustus, who promoted the fruit during the early Roman Empire, and to the Muses. But this 'muse' had in fact developed from the Arabic word *mouz*, a development from the earlier Sanskrit *moka*.

After the Classical period bananas reappeared in the Canaries and later in Europe in the early fifteenth century, brought from West Africa by the Portuguese, who used a variety of words from West and Central African languages – *banema, banana, bana* and *gbana*. The supposed first appearance of bananas in England, in a herbalist's shop in 1633, was amended by the discovery in 1999 of a banana skin in a Tudor rubbish deposit in London. The idea that 'going bananas' has some physiological link to the high amounts of sucrose and potassium in the fruit is unlikely.

**Cherry**. The absence of a Celtic or Germanic name for the cherry indicates that the tree was not native to north-west Europe; the Old English word *ciris* or *cirse*, found only in compounds like *cirisbeam*, meaning 'cherry tree', was replaced in Middle English by *cherie*, adopted from the Anglo-Norman and Old French *cherise*. It is thought that *cherie* was constructed as a singular from the mistaken idea that *cherise* was plural.

**Fig**. Reputedly imported by the Britons before the first Roman invasions, figs were known in England in the eleventh century; Ælfric, writing around the year 1000, translated the Latin *ficus* as *fic-wyrt*, which developed into *fike*. As disenfranchised English-speakers would have had less access to figs after 1066, this word disappeared from Middle English, superseded by French *figues*, imported for the tables of the wealthy. Valued for their high sugar content, eventually by the seventeenth century they were being grown in the Channel Islands, by which time they were called 'figges' or 'figs'.

**Fruit.** 'Fruit' derives via French from the Latin word meaning 'to enjoy'; thus fruits are literally the 'enjoyable or profitable products' of the plant. Several phrases, such as 'the fruits of your labour', indicate this, though in vegetable terms the definition is harder to fix. In terms of botany, law or cooking, certain foodstuffs, such as marrows, tomatoes and rhubarb, may be unexpectedly considered fruits or vegetables, implying that a fruit may be easier to recognise than to define.

**Gooseberry.** Gooseberries arrived in England in the 1530s, and sixteenth-century usage separated the word with a hyphen, or as two words – 'goose berry'. The fruit supposedly gained its name from being served as an accompaniment to goose, following the medieval custom of serving a sharp sauce or fruit with poultry. However, Smythe Palmer in *Folk Etymology* (1882) states that 'whatever be the origin of this word, … it certainly has no connexion with "goose"', and Skeat in *A Concise Etymological Dictionary of the English Language* (1882) prefers the idea of a corruption from *groise-berry*, meaning 'hairy berry'.

**Lemon.** The lemon appeared in English around 1400, as *lymon*. Johnson's derivation of the word from the 'low Latin' *limonium* fits with the generally accepted idea that Arabs introduced lemons to the Mediterranean world as late as the seventh century. The Arabic word transcribed as *lima* was hybridised with Persian to give *limun* – *lim* was the word for citrus fruits in Persian and Arabic, and, earlier, *nimbu* was the Sanskrit word for a 'lime'. The hybridised history of the word reflects the origin of the fruit; the hybrid of a citron and a lime was hybridised with a pomelo, a large citrus fruit, the ancestor of the grapefruit.

**Medlar.** The Old English name for 'medlar' was *openærs*, though opinion is divided on whether this description referred to the appearance or the effect of the fruit; terminology we would now class as rude, over-direct or offensive was to the Anglo-Saxons 'normal' language, whose status was debased after 1066, to the point where most of our swear-words are direct developments from Old English, with French-based polite forms. This is another aspect of the 'pork/swine' distinction. Though the Norman French dialect word for a 'medlar' was *cul du chien*, supporting the visual description claim, the *OED* quotes F. T. Elworthy in 1888 as writing: 'The fruit used medicinally is said to be aperient [laxative] …["open-ass" remains] the common and usual name among the working class.' The name 'medlar', documented from the early fifteenth century, derives from Old French.

**Orange**. Going by the changes in the words, the orange (as *naranj*) travelled from the Arabic world to Italy, where it became *arancio*, arriving in England as 'orange', where it is documented from around 1400. The 'n' was thus dropped from the word to the article long before it was adopted into English. These oranges were the bitter type, known eventually as 'Seville oranges' long after the sweet variety, called 'China oranges', were introduced by the East India Company in the seventeenth century. The mandarin and tangerine originate from China and Tangiers, but the clementine, originating from a chance hybridisation of a tangerine and a Seville orange, owes its name to the Latin word for 'mercy'.

**Pear**. The Latin word *pira* was adopted into Old English as *pere* or *peru*, developing into *pere* by 1300, and *peare* by 1470 (*Chambers Dictionary of Etymology*, 1988). 'Williams pears' were originally grown by a schoolmaster, John Stair, in 1770 but were renamed for sale (possibly someone realised that 'Stair pear' was not an ideal marketing choice); they are known as 'Bartlett pears' in America and Australia, Enoch Bartlett having bought the land on which the pears were first grown in Massachusetts.

**Pineapple**. In several languages the word for 'pineapple' derives from the Brazilian Tupi word *nana* or *anana*; but cultivation of the plant had spread from Brazil to the West Indies before the Spanish arrived and, when Columbus found it growing on Guadeloupe during his second voyage, his men called it *piña* on account of the fruit's similarity to a pine-cone. According to Davidson (2006), this gave rise to some misunderstanding in English sixteenth-century cookbooks, where 'pine apples' actually meant 'pine kernels', despite Walter Raleigh's promotion of the tropical fruit as 'the princesse of fruits'.

**Raspberry**. Webster believed 'raspberry' was derived from 'rasp', 'so named from the roughness of the brambles', while for Partridge (*Origins*, 1982) it was connected to Middle French *vin raspé*, deriving from the verb *rasper*, meaning 'to scrape'. While there may be a connection to a late medieval wine called *raspis*, for most authorities the etymology is left as 'unclear'. The earlier form of the word was *raspis*, with 'berry' added superfluously, perhaps to fit the pattern of 'blackberry' and 'strawberry'.

**Strawberry**. The 1867 *Chambers's Etymological Dictionary* proposes that the 'strawberry' is so called because it 'strews' or 'spreads' along the ground, echoing the implication of Ælfric's eleventh-century spelling, *streabarige*. The word is substantially different both from the Latin *fragaria* and forms in other Germanic languages. The Old English *streawberige* may come from the idea that the fruit may be found under mown grass (Webster, 1828), or from the hairlike strands covering the fruit (Weekley, *The Romance of Words*, 1912), or because it strays (Davidson, 2006). Most likely is that the sense of the earliest form was lost, and the first half of the word was replaced by the similar sounding 'straw', with the justification that to prevent its rotting the fruit is supported on straw.

# Vegetables

**Asparagus**. Webster supposed that 'asparagus' was derived from the Latin and Greek word for 'to tear', or from a word for 'spire', owing to the shape of the stem. The Medieval Latin form *sparagus*, found from around 1000, deriving from the Greek *asparagos* and Latin *asparagus*, became the English *sparage* between the fifteenth and seventeenth centuries. This in turn became 'asparagus' or 'sparagus', corrupted to 'sparrowgrass', which during the eighteenth century became the accepted form. During the nineteenth century 'asparagus' was re-established, 'leaving sparrow-grass to the illiterate' (*OED*).

**Bean**. 'Bean' comes via Middle English *bene* or *beene* and Old English *bean* from an early Germanic root-word that appears as similar words in Old Norse, Old High German and Old Frisian, and as *ffaen* in Welsh; these and the loose similarity to Old Slavonic *bobu* and Old Prussian *babo* and Latin *faba* support speculation that there was an Indo-European root-word *bhab*, which as it moved north-westwards developed a nasal second syllable. Johnson offered no etymology, neither did Webster, nor Lemon in 1783, beyond the Latin and Greek versions of the word. Beans have been a staple of the British diet probably since Roman times – the broad bean and the horse-bean (smaller and stronger-tasting, and used in falafel) were probably already being cultivated when the Romans arrived. Broad beans were known in the eighteenth and nineteenth centuries as 'Windsor beans', possibly in an attempt by cookery book authors to raise their status and increase usage. The American equivalent to the British 'broad bean' is 'fava-bean', an adoption from the Italian *fava*. Baked 'haricot beans' were effectively developed in Pittsburgh by Heinz in 1895 and, after an unsuccessful attempt in 1905, they were successfully marketed in Britain from the early 1920s. Before that there had been other bean imports from America: 'runner beans' were introduced by John Tradescant in the early seventeenth century, 'kidney beans' were noted in London in 1698 by Sorbière, and 'butter beans' were imported in the late nineteenth century.

**Broccoli**. The quotation from Pope in Johnson's entry for 'broccoli' implies that in the eighteenth century it was not a highly regarded food:

> 'Content I am with little, I can piddle here
> On broccoli and mutton round the year.'

Though broccoli is a diuretic, 'piddle' here means to 'while away time'. Until the twentieth century purple-sprouting broccoli was the dominant variety: when the green variety arrived in Britain it was known as 'calabrese' after its source, Calabria. The word is an Italian diminutive of *brocco*, meaning a 'shoot' or 'stalk'. With the exception of Hannah Glasse in 1747, who spelt it 'brockola', the spelling has remained fairly constant; Dods in 1826 and Kitchiner in 1823 used 'brocoli', but most dictionaries, including Johnson's (1755), Webster's (1828), Chambers (1972) and Collins (2007), stay with 'broccoli', the Italian version. The *OED* allows both spellings, though the Oxford-published *Modern English Usage* (1998) states that 'broccoli' with a double 'c' is 'now the only spelling'.

**Cabbage**. The cabbage and the kale are varieties of the same plant, but the tight-headed cabbage was not known in Britain until the sixteenth century, when it was brought from Holland. Middle English adopted the French word *caboche*, which ultimately derives from the Latin *caput*, meaning 'head'; this replaced 'cole-wort', a derivative from Old English which developed into 'kale', the loose-leaved vegetable.

**Carrot**. It is fairly clear that the word 'carrot' is derived from the French *carotte* and the Latin *carota*, and that the first use of the word in English, as 'karette', dates from the early sixteenth century. Ælfric around the year 1000 translated the Latin *cariota* as *waldmora* ('forest root'), and *daucus* (now used as the genus name) as *wealmora* ('foreign root'). Both of these words may have been used for carrot or parsnip; however, until the end of the medieval period in Britain the widely grown carrot was not a large succulent root, but a plant grown for its aromatic foliage and seeds. These were used medicinally. The other widely used term for 'carrot' during the Old English period was *wylisc moru* ('Welsh, i.e. foreign, root', contrasted with *englisc moru*, 'English root', or parsnip); this term appears only in leechdoms (medical guides) and the *Liber Medicinalis*. Carrot seeds were believed to be diuretic, contraceptive and stimulant, and the grated roots were used to soothe burns. The only documented appearance in text between 1066 and 1500 for anything that might be a carrot root is in a 1425 Latin/Middle English vocabulary, where *daucus* is translated as *clap-wype*.

The variety of carrot that produces the large root was brought west by Arabs, arriving in Spain, where it was first described in the twelfth century; from there cultivation spread throughout Europe, notably to Holland, from where the first orange carrots were introduced to Britain.

**Garlic, leek**. Garlic is a compound of two words, 'gar' meaning 'spear', and 'leek', and many texts up to the seventeenth century retained the spelling 'garleek'. Only Old Norse uses a similar construction, probably borrowing it from Old English; other Germanic languages have used other words such as 'bud' or 'white' together with 'leek' to make a compound word for garlic. This would seem to indicate that the leek was known in northern Europe before other onion-type plants, and that garlic, with its own name in southern Europe (variations on the Latin *allium*), was identified as one variation of a group of plants called 'leek'.

*Leac*, the Old English for 'leek', was applied to other plants of the onion family, including 'onion' itself and 'wild garlic' (*bradeleac*). The leek was in the post-Conquest period also called the *porret*, from the Latin *porrum*, until the Old English word reasserted itself from the fourteenth century: Chaucer's Summoner was partial to 'garleek, onions and eke lakes'. Garlic's role throughout history has often been medicinal, as its taste and smell have aroused strong feelings; John Evelyn in *Acetaria* (1706) described it as 'part of the punishment for such as had committed the horridest crimes'.

**Mushroom**. The Anglo-Norman and Middle English spellings *musseroun*, *musheron* and *musherom* derived from the Middle French *mouceron*, which developed from a Late Latin form *mussirion* or *mussarion*, which some authorities suggest may be connected to words for 'moss'. The Old English word for mushroom was *swamm*, though *musarion* was in use as an English word as early as the ninth century, according to Davidson (2006). It is supposed that mushrooms were not particularly favoured during the Anglo-Saxon and medieval periods, though they retained a medicinal use (a thirteenth-century glossary translates the Latin *fungus* as *wulvesfist*, indicating an awareness of their dangerous properties too), but *metteswam* in Ælfric's *Colloquy* shows that as *mette* they would have been eaten.

**Onion**. The onion was introduced to Britain by the Romans and quickly established itself as an important food and cultural item, featuring in a number of Anglo-Saxon riddles as *cipe* or *ciepe*, from the Latin *cepa*, which was replaced by the Anglo-Norman *ungeon*. The *OED* proposes the derivation from *unio*, a kind of single-shoot onion, described in a Classical Latin text, the word also being used to describe a large pearl.

**Pea**. In Old English a 'pea' was *piose*, with the plural form *piosan*; it had been acquired from the Latin *pisum* before the period of migration to Britain. In Middle English these converged to give variations on *pease* or *peese*, though the *Boke of Nurture* (1470) gives a recipe for 'bakon served with peson', a retention of the Old English plural ending with 'n', still retained in 'children'. The documentation of a singular form, 'pea', is surprisingly late – 1666 according to the *OED*.

Thus by the seventeenth century there existed a singular, 'pea', a plural, 'peas', and a word to describe the substance of a lot of them, 'pease', which was used in 'pease-porridge', 'pease pudding' and the often mis-spelt 'peasemeal'. 'Grey-pease', a flour made from ground dried peas, was a major constituent of the 'common people's food', according to Sorbière in 1698.

**Potato.** The 'grocer's potato' has become a byword for the confusion surrounding the use of the apostrophe, in this case probably emerging from uncertainty as to how to spell the plural form. The *OED* offers both 'potatoes' and 'potatos', describing the second as 'non-standard', rather than 'incorrect'. 'Potato' is from the Haitian word *batata*, which became *patata* in Spanish. The unpromising high-altitude plant *Solanum tuberosum* was taken by the Spanish from Peru (where it was called *papa*) to Europe, where it acquired a variety of names, based on 'earth apple' (*pomme de terre*) and 'earth truffle' (the Italian *tartufo bianco*, which developed into *taratufflo*, which became the German *Kartoffel* and the Russian *kartochki*). First documented growing in England in 1579, under the name of 'Virginia potato', it did not acquire its status as a basic food until the late eighteenth century, by which time the singular form was still being spelled 'potatoe'. The tuber rapidly grew in popularity, partly due to its versatility, until by the mid-nineteenth century sixty million baked potatoes were being sold every year on the streets of Britain; it is now the fourth most eaten foodstuff in the world. The nickname 'spud' developed in the mid-nineteenth century from the spade used to lift potatoes.

**Pumpkin.** Also known as the 'pompion' (Webster's preferred version in 1828, and the version given in Johnson's 1755 *Dictionary*) and 'pumpion' (Wolley, 1664), the word developed to 'pomkin' and 'pompkin' between the sixteenth and eighteenth centuries, and in the United States developed into 'punkin' (though the current 'correct' form is 'pumpkin' according to the *Oxford Dictionary of American Usage*, 1998). The earlier forms 'pompon' and 'pumpion' are closer to the Middle French root-word *pompon*, itself a development from the Tuscan *popone* and the Latin *pepo,* and the Greek *pepon*, meaning 'ripe'. In the sixteenth century 'pompions', newly introduced to Britain from France, were used to fill pies, a recipe that travelled to America with the early settlers. The connection to ripeness may be seen in the fact that the fruit is not eaten until visibly ripe, the stalk having dried and disconnected.

**Rhubarb**. Prized as an antidote to a choleric humour in the period of pre-scientific medicine, rhubarb is a leaf vegetable, but in 1947 the United States Customs Court in Buffalo, New York, ruled that as it was normally eaten as a dessert it was thus a fruit (Davidson, 2006). During the nineteenth-century Opium Wars, when China still exported dried rhubarb to Britain, it was in use primarily as a purgative; for a while the Chinese attempted to stop the supply in the hope of causing an epidemic of constipation. From the medieval period the long trade route from the east meant that it arrived via Europe; thus the name is derived from a number of European languages, Old French *rubarbe*, Spanish *ruibarbo* and Portuguese *rheubarbo*, from the Medieval Latin *rheubarbarum*. It is supposed that as the plants were said to have grown along the banks of the Volga, formerly called the Rha, its name has developed from *Rha-barbarum*, 'Rha of the barbarians'; alternatively, it comes from the Greek root-word *rhia*, meaning 'to flow'.

**Spinach**. Spinach was little known in Britain before the sixteenth century, having arrived in Europe with the Arabic settlers in the Iberian peninsula in the eleventh century. There were two words for the plant in Old French, *espinage* and *espinache*, which were reflected in the two simultaneous English spellings, 'spinage' and 'spinach', which existed up to the mid-nineteenth century. The route of the plant's travels has been used to support a derivation from the Arabic *isfinaj*, while others proposed that the Latin *spina* was a reference to the spiny seeds of some varieties.

**Vegetable**. In Old English, vegetables were either 'herbs', if the edible parts were leaves, or otherwise 'worts'. 'Vegetable' was used as an adjective, to mean 'living and growing, in the manner of a plant', from around 1400 and was not used as a noun for another 180 years. The use of the word to describe edible plants, particularly when cooked, is not documented before the mid-eighteenth century.

# Salad

**Avocado**. Rarely referred to now as an 'avocado pear', this fruit was first mentioned in English in 1672, favourably, though many later writers, including both Johnson and Webster, found it 'insipid'. The Spanish encountered it in Mexico, where in Nahuatl, the language of the Aztecs, they were called *ahuacatl*, meaning 'testicle'. This was hispanised as *aguacate* and as the existing word *avocado* (meaning 'lawyer'); these in turn became *aguacat* and *avocat* in French, and in English 'avigato', 'avogato' and even 'alligator-pear', a form used by Webster, and still in use in the United States in the late 1920s.

**Celery**. For Johnson, celery was a species of parsley, and the word can be traced back through French, Italian and Latin to the Greek word for the plant, *selinon* – the early-eighteenth-century spelling of *sellery* retained the connection. Wild celery, known as *smallage*, is documented from the thirteenth century, appearing first as *smallache* (*OED*), *ache* being an adopted French word which developed from the Latin and Greek *apium*, another word for 'parsley'. Until the mid-seventeenth century this wild celery was generally preferred to the cultivated plant introduced by the Romans. The Old English word for celery, *merece*, survived as *march* or *merche* until the seventeenth century and is similar to words for 'celery' in Danish, Swedish, Norwegian and Icelandic.

**Cucumber**. Despite the absence of archaeological evidence for cucumbers at Anglo-Saxon sites, there were at least three words in Old English for the plant: *eorthappel*, *cucumer* and *hwerhwette*. *Cucumer*, a direct adoption from Latin, would have travelled with clerics and, under the influence of French, became the dominant word from the fourteenth century; *eorthappel* is a fair description, bearing in mind the early meaning of 'apple' as any fruit. *Hwerhwette* is puzzling – *hwer* is Old English for a pot or cauldron; but in the fifteenth century another name appeared in a Latin/English pictorial vocabulary – *flage*. 'Cucumber' became the established word during the sixteenth century, with a variety of spellings, but the folk etymology spelling of 'cowcumers', with slight variations, became the established spelling for most of the seventeenth century. In 1669 Digbie spelt it 'cowcombers', and in 1698 Sorbière spelt it 'cowcumbers', but by 1728 (Eliza Smith's *The Compleat Housewife*) the spelling had reverted to 'cucumbers'.

**Lettuce**. Evelyn's praise for the lettuce ('It represses Vapours, conciliates Sleep, mitigates Pain') includes the story that the Emperor Augustus erected a statue and altar to the plant after its use cured him of 'a dangerous Sickness'; but Bailey warned that 'immoderate use of them is prejudicial to the eyesight and dampens the natural heat'. A Middle English word for 'lettuce', *slep-wurt*, goes against the expected pattern in which vegetables whose leaves were eaten were called 'herbs' rather than 'worts'. Old English words for lettuce were *thuthistel* and *leahtric*, but by the fifteenth century *letusa* was in use.

**Salad**. 'Salad' means 'salted', from Old French *salade* and Provençal *salada*. The word appeared in the *Forme of Cury* (1390) as *salat*, in which the dressing of oil, vinegar and salt was integral to the dish. Other spellings, 'salad' and 'sallet', developed, including 'sallat' in the sixteenth century. The *Forme of Cury* has a recipe for 'salat' with parsley, leeks, onion, garlic, mint, sage and other herbs, but by the early sixteenth century Catherine of Aragon had to send to Holland for salad leaves. During the seventeenth century salad vegetables were eaten either raw and dressed or boiled ('Divers Salats Boyled' appears in *A New Booke of Cookerie*, 1615); the practice of boiling survived into the eighteenth century.

The seventeenth century saw the regular appearance of salads on the table (Markham in 1623 gives recipes for 'some to furnish out the table, and some for both use and adornation'), the first recipe book devoted to salad, *Acetaria* by John Evelyn, and the appearance of 'grand sallets', which eventually developed into 'salmagundi', later 'Solomon Gundy', from the French *salmigondis*. This dish was a large salad containing a wide range of ingredients, including anchovies, herring, chicken, boiled eggs and pickles, whose changing recipes act as an indicator of the status of salad. Farley's 1783 'solomon gundy' contained few vegetables other than parsley (though it did feature a pineapple carved out of butter). Lettuce leaves appear in Glasse's 1747 'salamongundy', but nowhere in Kitchiner's 1823 *Cook's Oracle*. By the nineteenth century salads had fallen out of favour – Meg Dods in 1826 described them as 'a harmless luxury … affording little nourishment' and her 'salmagundi' contained no salad at all. 'Solomongundy' still survives in various places, notably Jamaica, but primarily as a fish recipe. By the time of Mrs Beeton's 1861 *Book of Household Management,* salads had returned to the dinner table.

**Tomato**. Tomatoes, native to Ecuador and Peru, arrived in England in 1597 but were used more as a decorative plant than a food source until the nineteenth century, often being known as 'love-apples'. Markham in 1625 called them 'apples of love', as opposed to 'marveilous apples' (those found on trees). Indeed the word 'tomato' was so unfamiliar that it does not feature in Johnson's 1755 *Dictionary* nor in the edition for 1790 (though that does have 'love-apple', defined brusquely as 'a plant'). The name 'love-apple' stuck to the tomato from its arrival until the mid-nineteenth century, when it was occasionally called 'tomata' (Eliza Acton, *Modern Cookery*, 1847); Kitchiner in 1823 gave a recipe for 'tomata or love-apple sauce'. By 1828 Webster had resolved that in the United States the fruit would be referred to as 'tomato, called sometimes the love-apple'.

# Meat

**Bacon**. Bacon, essentially the 'back' of the pig, was adopted in fourteenth-century English from the Old French *bacon*, itself a development from Medieval Latin *baconem*, from *baco*, adopted from a Germanic root-word meaning 'back'. The word was in use before the Norman Conquest, implying that it was probably brought to England following French-speaking Edward the Confessor's return from his youth spent in exile. The specific sense of a 'side of cured pork' came into use in the seventeenth century; previously 'bacon' was applied to pork, cured or not. A 'flitch' of bacon is an older word for a 'side of pork', from the Old English *flicce*, which Partridge (1982) links to the Old English *flæsc*, meaning 'flesh' or 'meat'. 'To bring home the bacon' dates from 1909.

**Beef**. 'Beef' was an Anglo-Norman introduction, adopted to indicate the meat, but also the animal. This seems to have happened with larger animals (pork, venison, mutton, beef), but not with smaller ones such as rabbits or poultry. *Bouf*, *boef* and *beef* replaced the Old English *cu* and *oxa* and were adopted from Old French *boef*, derived from the Latin *bovem* and the Greek *bous*. Given that 'beef' is used so often to show the class difference between Norman and Saxon, the word appeared in writing in a recognisably English text rather late, about 1300 according to the *OED* – and it is recorded in written French only from 1155 (*Larousse Etymologique*, 2001).

**Chicken**. The earliest definition in the *OED* for 'chicken' is 'the young of the domestic fowl; its flesh'. It is only since the nineteenth century that the word has been used to mean a chicken of any age, or its meat; before that the word used was 'fowl', which originally meant any bird, but gradually became more specific. Chickens or hens (the two words are used fairly indiscriminately when referring to the animals) are domesticated varieties of the *Gallus domesticus*, which probably came to Britain with the Celts, up to five hundred years before the Romans; currently about 175 varieties are domesticated. The Old English *cicen* should, by analogy with other words, have evolved into *chichen* but developed the hard middle consonant as in words for 'chicken' in Dutch and German; while 'hen', with its secondary meaning of the 'female of any species of bird', developed directly from the Old English *hen*, the feminine of *hanna*, meaning a 'cock' (Old English used *hen* where we would use 'chicken', as in 'henne broth', or 'chicken soup'). A 'capon', a castrated cock, favoured more in medieval times than now, was adopted from Latin before the Conquest, probably via French.

**Corned beef**. In North America the term 'canned pressed beef' is used for what is known in Britain as 'corned beef'. 'Corned beef' in the United States means what it used to mean in Britain, namely 'beef preserved by salting', using 'corns' or 'grains' of salt (the word 'corn' meaning 'any kind of hard grain'). Johnson's 1755 *Dictionary* gives the verb 'to corn', meaning 'to sprinkle with salt', while Kate Colquhoun in *Taste* (2007) points out that during the period of the First World War corned beef was often made at home. Nineteenth-century canned beef was evidently not so finely chopped as now; sold to the Navy, it was known as 'Sweet Fanny Adams', after a murder victim of 1867. The expression 'bully beef', often used as slang for 'corned beef', dates from the mid-eighteenth century and is derived from *boeuf bouilli*, meaning 'boiled beef' (*bouillir* also gave *bouillon*, a stock produced by boiling – British 'stock cubes' are American 'bouillon cubes').

**Ham**. 'Ham' comes directly from Old English, but Greek *kneme*, meaning the 'lower leg', is connected, and the *OED* suggests a Germanic root-word meaning 'to be crooked'. Curing by smoking and brining was practised in Europe before the Romans came to Britain, but the Latin word *poples*, meaning ham, did not influence the Germanic or Celtic vocabulary. 'Ham' was originally just the part at the back of the knee, and not limited to pork, and developed into meaning the whole of the leg during the sixteenth century; recipes before then tended to use the word 'pork' with instructions to *sethe* (boil) it, presumably to lose the saltiness. Some Old English dictionaries translate *flicce* as 'ham', but this would be more likely a large piece of bacon (a flitch).

**Hamburger**. Though recipes for chopped meat held together with egg and flour have been around for centuries (e.g. in Hannah Wolley, *The Accomplish't Lady's Delight*, 1675), the name 'hamburger' probably originated with German migrants to the United States in the mid-nineteenth century, possibly as a form of cooking steak on ships of the Hamburg Line, or because a majority of these migrants travelled via Hamburg. By the end of the nineteenth century the recipe was being heavily promoted in the United States by Dr J. H. Salisbury, as a result of which they were also known as 'Salisbury steaks', which name was widely supported during the First World War. By 1932 there were recipes for 'Hamburg steak', and the word 'hamburger' had come back into use; the differentiation between the home-made 'Hamburg steak' and the stall-sold 'hamburger' suggests that the word 'burger' had already acquired cheap fast-food associations.

**Lard**. 'Lard' is a versatile word. 'To lard' is found in English before 'lard' itself; a recipe in the *Forme of Cury* (1390) uses *white greece*. 'Larding' involved putting fat over a roasting dish and developed into the idea of laying one ingredient over another to flavour it – a nineteenth-century recipe for leg of lamb suggests 'larding' it with anchovies. 'Larding' was not limited to laying one thing over another – a 1920s American recipe involves 'drawing through poultry or meat thin strips of salt pork or bacon', using a 'larding needle'. Glasse in 1747 called these strips of meat 'lardoons'. 'Lard' is derived from the Old French word for 'bacon', which comes from the Latin *lardum*, meaning specifically 'bacon fat'. The corresponding Old English word, *rysle*, disappeared.

**Meat**. The Middle English *mete* developed from the Old English *mete* or *mæt*. This and similar words in other Germanic languages, together with words for 'animal feed' in Celtic languages, point to a common root. The *OED* proposes that the Latin *madere*, meaning 'to be wet, succulent or fat', would indicate an Indo-European root, which may have carried an idea of the desirability of cooked meat. That 'meat' was not limited to the bodies of animals can be seen from the use of the word *flæscmete* ('fleshmeat') in Ælfric's *Colloquy* of around 1000 – and 'white meat' later was used to describe dairy products. As late as 1470 *The Boke of Nurture* describes butter as 'an holsome mete, furst and eke last', and only from the fourteenth century did 'meat' gradually come to mean the 'edible flesh of animals'. A few phrases such as 'meat and drink' retain links with the former usage.

**Mutton**. 'Mutton', sheep meat older than one – sometimes two – years old, is one of the familiar three pairs of words that distinguished the Norman at his table from the Saxon in the field, who knew the animal as 'sheep' (though the pairing was not quoted by Walter Scott in *Ivanhoe*). Middle English *mouton* derived from the Old French *molton* or *multun*, meaning 'sheep', itself from the Medieval Latin *multo* and *multonem*, possibly from a conjectural Celtic root *mol-*, meaning 'to be gentle'. Mutton has lost its former status and has often provoked strong reactions: Fanny Cradock famously referred to it as 'divorce meat', while both Shakespeare and James Joyce linked it with prostitution. William Kitchener in 1817 declared that the finest mutton came from a five-year-old wether, in contrast to Pullar's contention that 'to mention mutton to a butcher is to see him react as though you had removed your knickers in his shop' (*Consuming Passions*, 1971). In 2004 the Mutton Renaissance Campaign was launched, but Davidson (2006) classes mutton as 'a rarity'; it remains to be seen how much longer Joyce's phrase 'mutton dressed as lamb' retains a recognisable frame of reference. 'Lamb' is Old English from the ninth century, previously *lomb*; the pronunciation of the 'b' disappeared during the Middle English period.

**Pork**. 'Pork' came as an Anglo-Norman introduction from the Old French *porc*, itself from the Latin *porcus*. The modern English word 'farrow' derives from the Old English *fearh*, meaning a 'piglet', which probably derives from a conjectural Germanic stem *farh-*, and further back an Indo-European stem *pork-*. By 1736 Bailey was using 'hog' as a chapter heading for pork recipes; Old English *hogg* possibly developed from a Celtic root and has been retained in the United States, while in Britain it is rarely used outside the meat trade.

**Rabbit**. A 'rabbit' was formerly the young of a 'coney' or 'cony'; 'cony' was from the Latin *cuniculus*, via Old French *conis*, while 'rabbit' can only be traced back to a possible Anglo-Norman *rabotte*. While 'cony' is now rarely used in Britain, in recipes before 1700 it was always used instead of 'rabbits'. The spelling 'rabbit' dates from the late eighteenth century, superseding 'rabbet'.

**Salami**. The first use in English of the word *salami* (an Italian derivation from the Latin for 'salted') is documented by the *OED* as in a book translated by an American, written by an Austrian about a journey to Iceland. In Charlotte Cooper's 1852 translation of Ida Pfeiffer's best-selling *Journey to Iceland*, the writer sees two people eating 'salami' in a theatre in Leipzig (the same word is used in the German of the original). *Salami* is properly a generic term for many kinds of salt-cured sausages, which have a history in Italy dating back more than two thousand years.

**Sausage**. The first recorded spelling (1450), *sawsyge*, shows a link to the Medieval Latin *salsicia* and the Old French *saussiche*, which is found in twelfth-century Anglo-Norman as *saucistre*; the spelling *sawcege*, found in 1615, shows a continuation of this. But in 1553 there appeared the spelling 'sausage', probably a constructed etymology to indicate something that has been salted, following the model of the word 'breakage'. Sausages were not made only in entrails – recipes in 1675 and 1728 show sausages being made by pressing meat into galleypots; and the Old English word, *gehæcca*, implies chopped meat, rather than meat stuffed into a skin. By the eighteenth century 'sausages' was an umbrella term, including 'linkes' and 'cervelas' (saveloys), but the word was not included in Johnson's 1755 *Dictionary*.

**Sirloin**. The story that a loin of beef was knighted by a king of England was credited first by Thomas Fuller in his 1655 *Church History of Britain* to Henry VIII, and eighty years later by Jonathan Swift to James I, and later still to Charles II. The story may thus be dismissed as folk etymology, though the joke has been extended to a 'baron' of beef, two sirloins served joined by the backbone. 'Sirloin' actually derives from the Old French *surloigne*, meaning 'above the loin'. The spelling 'sir-' appeared in the seventeenth century, but 'surloin' was still current in the eighteenth century, though it does not appear in Johnson's *Dictionary*. Sorbière described seeing on his visit to London in 1698 a sirloin 'so immense that a French Footman could scarce set it upon the Table'.

**Steak**. The Old Norse word *stik*, meaning a 'stick', led to the verb *stika*, meaning 'to impale', and in turn to *steik*, 'a piece of meat impaled on a stick for cooking', and *steikja*, meaning 'to roast meat on a spit'. This eventually became *styke*, the spelling found in the early fifteenth century, and not inappropriate for some current pronunciation. The expression *carbonado* for 'steak cooked on a gridiron' was current from the sixteenth to the nineteenth century and shows the influence of Spanish cooking on English cuisine.

**Veal**. The Anglo-Norman *vel* derived from the Old French *veel*, from the Latin *vitellus*, a diminutive form of *vitulus*, the word for both a 'calf' and the 'yolk of an egg'. It is first found in English in Chaucer's *Merchant's Tale*, about 1386 (*OED*), rather too late to support the Norman/Saxon linguistic divide argument (the Old English word for a calf was *cælf* or *cucealf*). In Britain the gelatinous stock derived from calves' feet was a popular ingredient in many recipes until the mid-twentieth century; 'calves' foot jelly' seems to be the only situation in which 'calf' is used instead of 'veal'. 'Veal' also gives the word *vellum* for the best-quality parchment, made from the stomach skin of a young calf.

# Fish and Shellfish

**Cod**. This name for a fish is known only in English and may come from the early use of 'cod' to mean 'bag'; perhaps *cotfish*, dating from 1273, were caught in a bag-shaped net. The first appearance as 'cod' is documented from a statute of 1357 describing 'les trois sortz de lob, lyng & cod', at a time when the use of Anglo-Norman was disappearing – the other two fish names here are Germanic rather than from French.

**Crab**. The Old English word *crabba* is related to many similar forms in Germanic languages which indicate an Indo-European root-word *grobh-*, meaning 'to scratch'. Crabs were credited with a sour disposition, possibly from their movements, which led to the association with disease, particularly 'cancer' (the Latin name for a 'crab'), and the sour-tasting 'crab-apple'.

**Fish**. The Latin *piscis*, meaning 'fish', developed into similar words over the range of Germanic and Celtic languages. In Old English its form was *fisc*, which developed into Middle English *fisc* and *fisch*, and thus to 'fish', by the thirteenth century. The range of fish eaten in earlier times included anything in water that could be caught – in Anglo-Saxon times people ate '*swa wylce swa on wætere swimmath*' ('whatever swims in water'). Medieval cookery books often have several recipes specifically for 'fyssh days', when it was not permitted to eat meat; but what qualified as fish would not meet modern criteria. Barnacle geese were supposed to grow from trees that stood by water, hanging by their beaks till they fell; those falling into water survived, while those that fell on land died. This bit of ritualistic folly allowed the medieval wealthy to pretend barnacle geese were fish, and thus to eat them with a clear conscience. Fish cookery developed its own vocabulary: 'fish-kettles' were in use from the seventeenth century, and in 1747 Glasse recommended cooks to 'have your Fish-slice ready' when frying fish, though that implement had existed as a *sclys* since the fifteenth century.

**Fish fingers**. Frozen cod sticks in batter were launched in Britain in 1955, following market testing as a control product to measure the viability of a similar product made from herring. 'Herring savouries' were sold in South Wales, while 'cod sticks' were sold in Southampton, the latter proving much more successful. The subsequent brand-name, 'battered cod pieces', was fortunately rejected in favour of 'fish fingers' following consultation with female workers at the Birds Eye factory in Great Yarmouth. The brand Birds Eye was initiated in 1929 following the purchase of General Foods, a company which owned the rights to the fast-freezing process patented by Clarence Birdseye, who had observed Inuit food-preservation methods in the early 1900s.

**Kipper**. The Old English form *cypera* developed into Middle English *kypre*, and 'kipper' by the sixteenth century. It is rare to find a word that Partridge (1982) has to list as 'of obscure origin', but that is the case with 'kipper', where two meanings overlap. Male salmon in the spawning season are known as 'kippers' from the hooked lower jaw called the 'kip'; but salmon (originally) and herring (mostly after 1800) are 'kippered', by being filleted and smoked. One possible explanation is that male salmon, emaciated but easy to catch after their exhausting reproductive endeavours, could be made more palatable by the 'kippering' process.

**Lobster**. One proposed history of the word 'lobster' is that the Latin *locusta*, meaning 'lobster' or 'locust', developed into the Old English *lopystre*, though the change from 'c' to 'p' is rare. More likely is that it developed from *loppe*, meaning 'spider'. The established form had been reached by 1390, though *lobstar* is found in the fifteenth century; and the confusion between a 'lobster' and a 'crayfish' (or *crevise* in the 1470 *Boke of Nurture*) lasted a long time.

**Mussel**. The current spelling was first used by Shakespeare in *The Tempest* in 1610 but did not become fully established until the late nineteenth century. *Muscle* or *musle* in Old English developed from the Latin word *musculus*, meaning both 'mussel' and 'muscle', with the literal meaning of 'little mouse'.

**Oyster**. The Old English *ostre*, plural *ostran*, was probably acquired by Germanic-speaking people from Latin before they migrated to England in the middle of the first millennium. The Anglo-Saxons had elaborate recipes for oysters – *osterhlafas* were loaves of bread hollowed out and stuffed with fat, eggs, herbs and oysters, a recipe that was still in use in the eighteenth century, and which developed into Soyer's recipe for 'oyster porridge', a dish for the poor, oysters being available for three shillings per thousand in 1847. The Latin *ostrea* derived from the same source as the Greek root *osteo-*, meaning 'bone'. Among the Middle English spellings recorded in the *OED* are *olstre*, *ostree*, *eystur* and *hoystyr*.

**Plaice**. The Old English word for a 'plaice' was *fage*, from which may have developed the now lost verb *fage*, meaning 'to deceive', the plaice's camouflage being a kind of deceit. 'Plaice', found as *plays* in 1267, developed from the Old French *plaïs*, from the Late Latin *platessa*, meaning 'any kind of flatfish'.

**Tuna**. *Tunnye* is recorded from 1530, an anglicisation of the Italian *tonno*, Spanish *atun* and Portuguese *ton*, all from the Latin and Greek *thunnus*. The form 'tuna' developed from the end of the nineteenth century. The overlap of scientific and non-scientific names is complicated in the case of tuna. *Bonito*, the Spanish common name for 'tinned tuna', in English applies to the species *Sarda sarda* but is also used for the striped or oceanic bonito, *Euthynnus pelamis*. Skipjack, *Katsuwonus pelamis*, is a member of the tuna family, while 'tuna' or 'tunny' refers to members of the *Thunnus* and *Euthynnus* (literally 'good tuna') genera. So the word 'tuna' is likely to refer to different fish in different parts of the world, even before the vagaries of bilingual dictionaries are considered.

# Dairy Produce

**Butter**. The Greeks used butter for medicinal rather than culinary purposes, and May butter was kept specially for this purpose in fifteenth-century England: the first documented use of *buteran* in the *OED* is in a Saxon medical document. As a food item, butter was used by the Celts but avoided by the Romans, used by the Saxons but at first avoided by the Normans, and popular again in the sixteenth century for making raised pies. The Greek *bouturon* developed into the Latin *butyrum*, which developed into variations on *boter* or *buter*. The *OED* states that the Greek *bouturon* is usually supposed to be from *bous*, meaning 'cow', and *turos*, meaning 'cheese', but that the word 'is perhaps of Scythian or other barbarous origin', an idea that Partridge (1982) found 'unconvincing'. Bailey (1736) used the word to mean any sort of beaten paste.

**Cheese**. Germanic speakers adopted the Latin *caseus* and brought it to England, where it developed into Old English *cese* or *cyse* and Middle English *chese*. The importance of regional varieties of cheese can be seen in early marketing: Stilton cheese was not made in Stilton, but at Quenby, 30 miles away, but was sold where travellers would be more likely to buy it, at the Bell Inn in Stilton, on the Great North Road (not that the recipe was protected – Bailey gave an 'easy' version of it in 1736). Regional names of cheeses have developed a vocabulary that spreads beyond the site of origin: while some names are protected as guarantees of local manufacture, others such as Camembert or Brie are widely applied. 'Cheddar' as a name for cheese is best understood as a method of cheese-making that is carried on in many places far from Somerset; 'cheddaring', the process of cutting and layering the slabs of curd, is documented from 1909 (*OED*). 'Cottage cheese' first appeared in the United States, synonymous with 'smear-case', an anglicisation of *smierkase*, a Pennsylvania Dutch importation, indicating that the prime attribute of this cheese was that it could be spread on bread. 'Cheese' or 'curd', a conserve of egg and lemon or other ingredients, dates from the sixteenth century.

**Egg**. Toussaint-Samat wrote that King Louis XV of France ritually, and in front of an audience, every Sunday ate boiled eggs, removing the top of each one with a single swipe of his fork, preceded by the call 'The King is about to eat his egg!' 'Egg' derives from the Old Norse *egg*, though the Old English *æigh* survived as *ei* (plural *eyren*) beyond the fourteenth century; it even appears alongside 'egg' in Mulcaster's *Elementarie* (book on spelling) in 1582. The recipe for 'scrambled eggs' came later, first appearing in a French cookery book in 1784, though the first documented use in the *OED* is dated to eighty years later; this would make it the first use of the word 'scramble' in the sense of to 'take apart or muddle'. The 'yolk' of an egg derives from *ghealeye*, the Old English for 'yellow'.

**Margarine**. Margarine was invented directly as the result of a competition. The French Emperor Napoleon III challenged scientists to invent a butter substitute that would be suitable for the navy and the less well-off, and in 1869 Hippolyte Mège-Mouries synthesised 'margarine' from beef fat, skimmed milk and cow's udder. Two rival stories explain the name. Either the surface of the mixture had a sheen resembling the surface of pearls, so the name *margarin* was manufactured from the Greek *margaron*, meaning a 'pearl' (*marguerite* in French); or it was influenced by the name 'margaric acid', a supposed fatty acid, discovered by Chevreul in 1813, which left iridescent deposits like mother-of-pearl.

The original name was 'oleo-margarine', still used in the United States, though sometimes shortened to 'oleo'; but it was marketed in Britain originally as 'butterine', which provoked heated questions in the Houses of Parliament, at a time when the adulteration of manufactured food was rife. In a debate in July 1887 Lord Denman reported that 'the article was sold in Lancashire as "rine" and bosh, and in America it had been called bogus.' Though the 'correct' pronunciation of 'margarine' is with a hard 'g', this indicates that the invented word was not entirely appropriate, as it is almost always pronounced with a soft 'g'.

**Milk**. The Old English forms *meolc* and *milc* were similar to many Germanic words for 'milk' and developed into 'milk' during the fourteenth century. The Roman critical view of Celts as 'milk-drinkers' has been repeated in encounters between different cultures throughout history – the first Europeans to visit Japan were thought repellent as they smelled of old butter. In Britain until the nineteenth century milk was considered suitable only for invalids and children, though given the nature of urban dairying from 1700 onwards it was probably advisable not to drink milk at all. Though there was no Latin form similar to *milc* describing the substance, the Old English forms *milcian* and *melcan*, meaning 'to milk', were similar to the Latin and Greek verbs *mulgere* and *amelgein*, suggesting an Indo-European root-word *melg-*.

**Yoghurt**. *Yoghurd* appeared in English in 1625, with the spelling 'yogourt' appearing in 1687. The word was adopted from the Turkish yoğurt, originally 'sour fermented milk'. The *OED* gives only the spelling 'yogurt', with 'yoghurt' given as an alternative in the *Collins Dictionary* (2007), while *Chambers Twentieth Century Dictionary* (1972) gives 'yoghourt' and 'yoghurt'.

# Cereals

**Biscuit**. Johnson pointed out that 'biscuit' clearly denotes how the object described is made – *bis cuit* in French means 'twice cooked'. 'Biscuit' or 'biscuits' have a long and complex history, the Italian *biscotto* coming through Old French to Middle English as *besquite,* changing to *bisket*, and then back to 'biscuit', a final spelling change which the *OED* describes as 'senseless'. The term has included 'ship's biscuit' (or 'hard-tack'), 'Garibaldi biscuits' (apocryphally named after an incident when the Italian patriot accidentally sat on an Eccles cake during a visit to England in 1854), 'jumbles' or 'jumballs' (seventeenth-century knot biscuits, and the first use of 'jumble' as a noun), and Wolley's 1675 'French bisket', baked with coriander and aniseed to be 'kept in Boxes all the year', and 'Naples bisket', made with 'almonds and pine apple seeds' (probably pine kernels). The terminology is confusing: Markham's 1623 'bisket bread' and Bailey's 1736 recipe for 'spunge biscuit' both describe cakes, and there is a difference between Britain and the United States, where biscuits are savoury and cookies (from the Dutch *koekje*) are sweet. As Webster noted, 'the compositions under this denomination are very various.'

**Bread**. The success of wheat is largely based on its high gluten content, allowing the more efficient trapping of yeast-produced gases within the dough that becomes bread, a food so essential to society that the word 'company' means 'bread with'. The idea of fermentation links 'bread' to 'brew', and the word 'bread' has remained unchanged since Old English; however, a more common word in pre-Conquest England was *hlaf*, which became limited to the usage of 'loaf'. What we have lost are the names of many kinds of loaf: the late medieval *cantel of brede* (a chunk); small loaves called an *oblys* or *painmain* ('hand-bread'); tough bread made with any available cereals or legumes, called *maslin*; and *manchet*, made from fine white flour, and the lower-quality *cheat*. By 1736 Bailey was already praising French bread and recommending it for recipes such as 'lobster-loaves', bread hollowed out and stuffed with lobster meat.

**Bun**. 'What is that delicious little cake?', Queen Victoria is said to have asked on first seeing a penny bun. There is a possibility that 'bun' derives from the Old French *bugne*, meaning a 'swelling', which may also have been used to mean an 'airy cake'; but the first recorded use of the word in England is in a 1371 legal document defining the weights of kinds of bread. The sentence in Latin describes a loaf '*vocato* "'*bunne*"' (called 'bun'), indicating that it would be unknown by some. Partridge (1982) links it to the Gaelic *bonnach*, modern Scottish 'bannock', and there is also a similarity to the Spanish *buñuelo*, meaning a 'doughnut'.

**Cake**. Though the legend states that King Alfred allowed some cakes to burn while planning how to overcome the Danes, *kake* was probably adopted from Old Norse, ousting the Old English *cœcel* (there also existed an Old English word *crompeht*, which developed into 'crumpet'). In the seventeenth century some cakes were huge and heavy; 'pound cakes' used a pound each of butter, flour, sugar and eggs. But the following century saw the introduction of beaten eggs into cake recipes to make 'spunges'.

**Cereal**. 'Cereal' may mean either the seeds of wheat, rye, oats, etc – a word invented in the nineteenth century, and deriving from Ceres, the Roman goddess of agriculture – or, more commonly, a breakfast food. The second usage dates from the end of the nineteenth century, when proprietary foods, such as Granola and Grape-nuts, which had been developed initially by dieticians and vegetarians in the United States, were successfully marketed more widely. In Britain these were still perceived as foreign foods until the 1920s; in 1930 Jekyll recommended 'American cereals such as post-toasties, honey-grains, puffed wheat, or puffed rice'. Kellogg's registered the name Toasted Corn Flakes in 1907.

**Crumbs**. In a fifteenth-century vocabulary the word *crwme* means 'the inner part of the loaf', but the Old English *cruma* was used in the same way as the modern 'crumb'; the two concepts existed within the same word until the nineteenth century. The final 'b' began to appear in the written form in the sixteenth century, analogous to many words ending in 'mb' with a silent 'b'; the *OED* suggests that the 'b' appeared first in the derivative word 'crumble' and spread later to 'crumb'. The alternative spelling 'crum' continued in use into the nineteenth century.

**Flour**. The use of the word 'flower' to describe 'the best, the pick, the ideal' dates back to the thirteenth century and was also applied to ground wheat, as the 'flour or flower of meal', when the bran was separated. From the fourteenth century the spelling 'flour' has been in use, but 'flower' was also used until the eighteenth century; some cookery writers, such as Hannah Wolley, made the difference clear, having to use both flowers and flour in recipes. The distinction between the two spellings and usages became fully established only in the nineteenth century.

**Maize**. Maize is recorded in the sixteenth century, first as the Spanish form, *maiz* or *mais*, of a Cuban word *mahiz* or *mahis*, though by the seventeenth century direct contact between English colonists and indigenous people in North America led to the name 'Indian corn'. Unsuitability as a crop for much of Britain, and unfamiliarity with how to cook it, appropriately led to its being labelled with names that indicated foreignness – 'Spanish corn', 'Turkey-wheat', 'Guinea corn'. The term 'sweetcorn' developed in the seventeenth century in North America, where English-speakers were less wary of it. In America the word 'corn' alone has been used since the early eighteenth century, and 'sweetcorn' ('sugar corn' or 'American sweet corn' in Jekyll, 1930) was used for a particular variety; in Britain 'maize' is largely the name for a kind of animal feed. 'Indian meal poullenta' was suggested by Alexis Soyer in 1847 as a nutritious meal for London's poor, made from corn meal (the ground grain), rather than cornflour, which is flour made from maize with all the gluten and bran removed. Mary Byron's *Ration Book* (1918) gave several recipes using maize, including 'its preparations, hominy, semolina, maize-meal and flaked maize'. 'Hominy', from the indigenous American *auhuminea* meaning 'parched maize', is now seldom used in Britain; while 'semolina', a diminutive of the Italian *semola*, meaning 'bran', comes from wheat rather than maize.

**Noodles**. 'Noodle', which is first recorded in English from 1779, derives from the German *nudel*, which itself probably derives from *knödel*, meaning 'dumpling'. Chow mein, Chinese fried noodles, is a fairly accurate transliteration of the Chinese usually transcribed as *ch'ao mien*. A fourteenth-century British recipe for fried batter directs the cook to 'put they hond in the batere and let him renne down by they fyngerys, into the chafere'; the batter mix was eggs, flour, sugar, yeast and salt, and the hands had to be dipped into this mixture so that it ran off the fingers into the frying pan.

**Oats**. 'Oatmeal forms a considerable and very valuable article of food for man in Scotland, and every where oats are excellent food for horses and cattle.' With these words Webster cleverly alluded to Johnson's famous definition and also showed himself in a more generous light. The Old English word was *ate*, which developed into Middle English *ote*; no other Germanic languages have a similar word, though Partridge (1982) points out Lettish *auza* and Old Slavonic *ovisu*, which may be developments from the Latin *avena*.

**Porridge**. 'Porridge' was originally *porree*, a broth made from leeks, deriving from Old French; this is thought to have influenced the Anglo-Norman *potage*, producing the form 'porage', which eventually became 'porridge' in the sixteenth century. The association with cooked oats comes from the mid-seventeenth century but has been by no means exclusive. Just as cooked oatmeal has other names (such as 'stir-pudding', in the mid-twentieth-century Midlands), 'porridge' has meant 'Christmas pudding' ('plum-porridge' in Sorbière, 1698) and an eighteenth-century pudding made from broth, currants, spice, sugar, claret, sherry, oranges, lemon juice, prunes and biscuits.

**Rice**. For Johnson and Webster, 'rice' came to English from the Greek and Latin *oryza*, which became the Italian *riso*, and the French *ris* or *riz* (the Portuguese and Spanish versions, *arroz*, developed from the Arabic *arruz*, travelling from the Greek source on a clockwise journey round the Mediterranean). When *rys* appeared in Middle English in the thirteenth century it began to displace an Old English word, *hris*, which also developed into 'rice', meaning 'twigs' or 'brushwood', which now is more or less obsolete. Until the development of efficient strains of wheat, rice, together with maize, was the most efficient food produced by humans. Webster reckoned that 'it seems intended by the wise and benevolent Creator to be the proper food of men in warm climates'; however, the word does not appear in the text of the 1611 Authorised Version of the Bible.

**Spaghetti**. When Eliza Acton in 1849 introduced 'sparghetti' to Britain, as 'Naples vermicelli', it was a fairly recent word in Italian. The spelling showed the derivation of the word to be a diminutive of *spargo*, meaning 'cord'. Though the form 'spaghetti', introduced in 1888, became the accepted form in the UK, both spellings have been retained in Italian.

# On the Table

**Carve**. The *Boke of Keruynge*, published by Wynkyn de Worde in 1513, instructs the reader in the language of carving individual meats at the table. Among these, he is required to: 'spoyle that henne, fruche that chekyn, unlace that conye, dysplaye that crane, dysfygure that pecocke, untache that curlewe, alaye that fesande, chyne that salmon, undertraunche that purpos, and tayme that crabbe'. Some of these sound like the simple fun of word-making, while the unlikely operation of having to 'undertranch a porpoise' on the dining table seems to call for some kind of engineering skills. The list ends with the satisfied note 'Here endeth the goodly terms'.

Given that the first documented use of *unlace* in this sense appears in the fourteenth-century courtly romance *Sir Gawain and the Green Knight* (*OED*), it may be supposed that several of these terms arose in the fantasies of courtly love. The Old English *ceorfan*, meaning 'to carve', is similar to many northern European words for 'to notch or cut', and the Germanic root is thought to be linked to the Greek *graphein*, meaning 'to scratch or engrave'. The use of the term 'carver' for the chair at the head of the table for the person who carves the meat dates from the 1920s, while the first 'carvery', dating from 1962 (*OED*) was a buffet-style restaurant where patrons carved their own meat from a joint.

**Cup**. The Old English *cuppe* was adopted from the Late Latin *cuppa*, which provided similar words in both the Germanic and the Romance languages. The Old French form *coupe* was adopted into Middle English as *coupe* or *cowpe*, but as well as the continued Old English form there was also a Middle English *coppe*, which may have been a mixture of *cuppe* and *coupe*; only *cuppe* survived into Modern English, with the modern spelling appearing in the sixteenth century.

**Dish**. The Old English *disc* and later Middle English *dysche* was a development from the Classical Latin *discus* meaning a 'discus' or rarely the 'disc of a sundial', which had been adopted by Germanic speakers before they arrived in England. From the same root-word come the words 'dais' and 'desk', via the Late Latin development of *discus* to mean 'table'. It was not until the sixteenth century that the word was used to describe 'any particular kind of food' (Johnson, 1755).

**Fork**. Forks were first introduced into western Europe in the tenth century, but took another six hundred years to reach Britain from Italy, via France. This did not mean that until then eating was necessarily a messy affair: Chaucer's Madame Eglantyne in the late fourteenth century ate with her fingers, but 'let not a drop or a crumb fall on her clothes'. The Old English *forca* derived 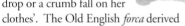 from the Latin *furca*, acquired during the period AD 450 to 650, and similar forms are found in Germanic and Romance languages.

**Glass**. The use of 'glass' to mean a 'drinking glass' is thought to date from around 1200. The Old English *glæs* derived from a Germanic root-word meaning 'to shine', which developed into similar words in most northern European languages, and also developed into the Old English word for 'amber', *glær*, and the word 'glare'.

**Jug**. 'Jug' appeared quite late, in Thomas Elyot's 1538 *Latin Dictionary* (the first to be printed in England) as '*Cantharus* – a pot or a jugge'; but there is no generally accepted idea of where it came from. Wedgwood suggested that it was a transference of 'Jug' as a familiar form of the name Joan (apparently a frequent name among servants – as in Shakespeare's 'greasy Joan'). Donald (1867) is one of the few etymologists to suggest a clear derivation, from the Old English *ceac*, meaning 'basin, cup or pitcher' – the first consonant would have been sounded as in modern 'ceiling'. Smythe Palmer (1882) pointed out that the slang use of 'jug' for 'prison', mostly found in Scotland, derives not from the shape of a jug, but from the Latin *jugum* meaning a 'yoke', of the sort used to harness oxen to a plough or cart.

**Knife**. By about 1300 the Old English *cnif* had become *knif*, having been adopted probably in the eleventh century from the Old Norse *knifr*. The 'k' sound at the beginning lasted in some areas until the seventeenth century.

**Plate**. The idea that seems to lie behind various words such as the Medieval Latin *plata* and the Old French *plate* is the idea of a flat piece of metal. In many languages, such as Old Icelandic or Old Swedish, this developed to mean 'chest armour', which appears in English as 'breastplate'. In Anglo-Norman 'plate' was used to mean a food dish from as early as 1117, alongside other words such as *dobler*, used in the fifteenth century, and 'trencher', documented from the fourteenth century but now used only as a conscious archaism.

**Saucer**. The first use of 'saucer' to go with 'cup' dates from the beginning of the eighteenth century, though the word *sawser* had been used as a receptacle for sauce since the thirteenth century. The first description of 'unidentified flying objects' as both 'saucers' and 'flying saucers' dates from 1947.

**Table**. The Old English *tæfel* was a 'gaming board', probably from the Latin *tabula*. This developed into *tabele*, merging with the Old French *table*, also from *tabula*, to give 'table' by 1200. The sense of a 'board on legs' dates from around 1300.

**Tureen**. The exotic-sounding tureen is a development from the humble *terrine*, a large earthenware pot, from the Latin *terra* meaning 'earth'. The French *terrine* became the English 'terrene' at the beginning of the eighteenth century, the change of spelling from 'ter-' to 'tur-' possibly influenced by the spelling of the place-name Turin. The word became more common as dinner services became available to middle-class households. By 1840 a 'tureen' had grown from a simple earthenware dish to a decorated china bowl with handles and a lid, but prior to this would have been small enough to be used for sauce – Kitchiner (1823) gives a recipe for 'Wow Wow sauce' (involving walnuts, pickled cucumbers, mustard, vinegar, and mushroom ketchup) to be eaten with 'Bouilli Beef', served in a 'sauce-tureen'.

# Dishes

**Beef olives**. This familiar English dish, made from strips of beef wrapped around a stuffing of onion, breadcrumbs and herbs, has nothing to do with olives. The name is another case of an attempt to make sense in English of a name that was comprehensible in Middle English, in this case *boeuf aloes* or *allowes*. *Allowes* was a medieval dish in which veal strips were wrapped around forcemeat, looking similar to cooked *alous* (larks); thus *beef allowes* was a cheap version of braised larks. The name 'beef olives' was established in the seventeenth century, but the link to larks was retained, probably by chance – Meg Dods's 1826 recipe recommends that beef olives should be roasted using a 'lark spit', a small spit designed for use in cooking small birds.

**Chips**. The strip of potato fried in oil, known in Britain as the 'chip', in the United States as the 'fry' or 'French fry', and in New Zealand as the 'hot chip', has provided fertile ground for researchers of food history. The word appears fairly early in recipe books: Bailey (1736) gave a recipe for 'China chips', candied orange or apricot peel. The creation of the chip was less an epiphany than a gradual process – in 1783 Farley gave a recipe for sliced potatoes fried until brown (see **crisps**), while Wolley in 1675 proposed half-inch slices of sweet potatoes fried in butter and vinegar. John Ayto (1993) points to Dickens's *Tale of Two Cities* (1859), with 'husky chips of potatoes, fried with some reluctant drops of oil', while Davidson (2006) prefers an eighteenth-century French origin, though quoting a Belgian claim for the invention of chip stalls in the 1860s. By 1870 the word 'chip' was fully established in Britain, with 'fish and chips' spreading from Lancashire in the 1880s. Mrs Beeton (1861) described the hot-fat frying process as 'Fried Potatoes (French fashion)', a term whose first use in the United States is widely ascribed to an O. Henry story from 1894, while a recipe in a leaflet from the Patriotic Food League (Scotland) (1917) uses very thin sliced potatoes, deep-fried twice, calling them 'chips'.

During the American-led invasion of Iraq in 1994, American resentment at French disapproval was seen in the way some establishments replaced 'French fries' with 'freedom fries' (similarly during the First World War 'hamburgers' had been replaced with 'Salisbury steaks', and 'German measles' with 'liberty measles').

The word 'chip', meaning a 'fragment of wood or stone cut off from a larger piece', dates back to 1300 but is connected to the conjectural Old English *cippian*, meaning 'to hit'.

**Chop suey**. 'Chop suey' was widely believed to have been invented by Chinese immigrants in San Francisco towards the end of the nineteenth century. The myth proposes that a Chinese cook required to provide food at a time when the usual ingredients were unavailable put together a mixture which was fortunately acceptable, indeed instantly popular; when asked its name, he said 'odds and ends', *tsap sui* in Cantonese. In fact, though the anglicisation of the pronunciation from Cantonese is correct, the recipe was a common rural dish from Toisan, from where many Chinese migrated to California. By the 1920s 'American chop suey' was a familiar recipe across the States, with the Chinese ingredients replaced by ones of European or American origin.

**Haggis**. Bag puddings of offal and cereal for preserving and transporting meat are by no means exclusive to Scotland – an English fifteenth-century cookbook gives a recipe for 'Hagws of a Schepe', meat and spices in 'the grete wombe of a Schepe', and a 1425 vocabulary has an entry for *hagase*. The word may come from a conjectural Germanic form *hakkon*, meaning 'to hack', which forms the base for similar words in several north-west European languages in the first millennium; but an Old Norse word *höggva*, meaning 'to hack', is proposed by Partridge (1982) as leading to the Scottish *hag* and *haggle*, meaning 'to cut' (Wyld, 1936, and Skeat, 1882, agree with this). C.T. Onions (1966) suggested a possible link with Old French *agace*, 'magpie', while Johnson (1755), spelling the word *haggess*, suggested a link with 'hog' and 'hack'. The variable and mysterious etymology seems to reflect the identity of the pudding's contents.

**Hodge-podge**. This is a dish that may have been named twice, or, like a river, has gathered tributary words into it. 'Hodge-podge' appears in *The Forme of Cury* as *hoggepot* (possibly an early rationalisation of the word as a 'pot big enough for a pig', just as a 'casserole' can be both a design of pot and a kind of dish); it was later spelt *hogpoch* and *hogepotche*. Colquhoun (2007) describes it as a late Tudor development from the Spanish *olla podrida*, with an interim stage *olepotridge*, the name used by Markham in 1623; it is more likely that a group of similar names already existed for a widely used dish, and *olla podrida* was assimilated into them. In the fifteenth century a *hodgepodge* was 'a confused mixture', applied not only to food, and this application sat side by side with the name of the recipe for at least two hundred years. Some of the recipes certainly were confused mixtures – Markham's 'olepotridge' had forty-five ingredients, including sparrows, blackbirds, fallow deer, half a pig, strawberry leaves and potato roots. In the eighteenth century its spelling became established as 'hodgepodge' or 'hodge podge', though in Scotland the form 'hotchpotch' was retained (Dods, 1826). Johnson (1755) attempted to trace the history of 'hodge-podge' back through the French *hochè pochè* and *hochepot* to *hachis en pot*, meaning 'minced meat in a pot', but *hachis* postdates the fourteenth-century English recipe for *hochepoche*. The idea of a jumble of anything to hand thrown into a pot may have given rise to a new word that seemed just right. Possibly the resulting dish also came out well, possibly not.

**Kebab**. *Kebab* is Turkish for 'meat', and *shish* for 'skewer'; thus using the word *kebab* for anything stuck in a faintly exotic combination on a skewer is based on a mistaken application of English word order to a Turkish phrase. The first use documented in the *OED* is dated 1813, but the earlier anglicisation, 'cabob', noted from 1673, was a development from the Arabic, Farsi and Urdu *kabob*, meaning 'roast meat' ('kabob' is still the preferred spelling in the United States). Farley (1783) gives a recipe for 'mutton kebobed', mutton spit-roasted with pickles for garnish. *Kabab* in Medieval Arabic always meant 'fried meat', and the transference of the word to 'grilled meat' seems to have occurred with the rise of the Ottoman Empire.

**Omelette**. In *Chambers's Etymological Dictionary* (1867) it is proposed that 'omelette' or 'omelet' derives from the French *oeufs mêlés*, meaning 'mixed eggs', a proposal supported by the Middle French spellings quoted by the *OED*, *œufmollette* and *œufmelete*. Partridge (1982) traced the Early Modern French *omelette* or *aumelete,* with the influence of the Latin *ovum*, meaning 'egg', back to the Medieval French *amelette*; this, by transference of consonants, had developed from the earlier *alumette*, deriving ultimately from the Latin *lamina*, meaning a 'thin layer'. The 2007 *Collins English Dictionary* adds that *alumette* developed from *alumelle*, meaning a 'sword blade'. 'Omelette' appeared in English as late as the early seventeenth century, when omelettes of puréed apple were made, but omelettes of herbs, vegetables and even sweet ingredients are recorded from Anglo-Saxon times; the word used was *æggemang*, literally an 'egg-mix'. The idea of cooking both sides of the omelette by slipping it over in the pan proved difficult for cooks in the seventeenth and eighteenth centuries, who were recommended to hold a hot fire shovel over the top. In the late medieval period omelettes were often flavoured with tansy, a bitter herb, to the extent that a 'tansy' became the accepted word for an omelette well into the eighteenth century.

The United States spelling is 'omelet', following Webster, while in Canada and Australia 'omelette' is preferred. But the spelling in Britain has embraced 'omelette' (Kitchiner, 1823), 'omelet' (Bailey, 1736; Dods, 1826; Jekyll, 1930), and 'omlet' (Acton, 1847; Evelyn, 1706), and both 'omelette' and 'omelet' (Donald, 1867; Wyld, 1936). For a while in the seventeenth and eighteenth centuries the word was spelt using variations on 'amulet', possibly folk etymology, possibly a mishearing: in 1664 Wolley used 'amalet', and Farley in 1783 used the spelling 'amulet' – Glasse also thirty-five years earlier had an 'amulet', but it was made with beans and cream, not eggs. The *OED* currently recognises only 'omelette', while Collins (2007) allows 'omelet' also.

**Pastry**. 'Pastry', both the word and the mixture, is formed from 'paste', a French word that appeared as the Anglo-Norman *past* or *paste*, meaning 'dough' or 'pastry', lasting into the sixteenth century as *paest*. These may go back to an early Medieval Latin word for a medicinal paste, and the Greek *pastai*, meaning 'barley porridge', which also developed into 'pasta'. Though pastry-cases were at first used primarily to keep cooked meats fresh, certain types, such as 'puff paste', documented from the sixteenth century, would have been eaten; and the 1545 *New Boke of Cockerye* includes a recipe for 'short paest for tart', with butter, sugar and saffron, certainly not intended for storage and disposal. For Bailey (1727) a 'pastry' was 'a Place where pastery Work is wrought; also Pies, etc., made of Paste'. The use of 'paste' for 'pastry' has been retained in North America. 'Pasty', also deriving from 'paste', is defined by Johnson (1755) as 'a pie of crust raised without a dish'. A 'patty', known first from the word 'pattypan' in the seventeenth century, was a small pie, and as late as 1936 synonymous with a 'pâté'; however, the word 'pâté', meaning a 'paste of meat and/or vegetables', was in use in Britain from the end of the nineteenth century.

'Filo' pastry ('phyllo' in the United States) derives from the modern Greek word for *a leaf*, but the metaphor may have been around for some time; the 1390 *Forme of Cury* includes a recipe with sheets of thin pastry called *foyles*, described as being 'as paper'. The connection between 'folio', a sheet of paper, and 'leaf' comes through the Latin *folium*, meaning 'leaf'.

**Pie**. 'Pye', in a Medieval Latin document dating from 1304 (*OED*), may come from the Medieval Latin *pia*, meaning 'pie' or 'pastry'; Johnson proposed that, as early pies were layers of pastry doubled over, the Latin *pie*, meaning 'foot', was a reasonable derivation. Partridge (1982) suggests that the word comes from one of the recipe's early ingredients, the magpie. What is clear is that early pies, usually in pastry raised by using dough with water, were primarily ways of cooking one thing inside another – a recipe for a thirteenth-century 'Grete Pye' has a small bird inserted into a larger one, and these inserted into another. A pie was essentially a method of cooking and preservation; the case, until the eighteenth century called a 'coffin' (essentially a box – the term is still used in a similar way in pilchard processing), allowed the cooked juices to be poured away and replaced with clarified butter, which would preserve the cooked meat for months, with the case being eventually discarded.

'Great pies' continued into the seventeenth century – Digbie (1669) offers 'humble pie' made from deer entrails, or 'umbles' (becoming 'humble pie' in the nineteenth century), while Markham (1623) mentions pies made with porpoise and elk. In the eighteenth century there appeared layered pies of meat and vegetables, called 'puptons' or 'pulpatoons', from the French *poupton*; and 'pudding pies', a term used in various ways – for Johnson it meant a 'pudding with meat inside'.

**Pudding**. A conjectural Indo-European root-word *put*, meaning 'to swell', is the probable basis for words in several Celtic languages, such as Welsh *poten*, meaning 'intestine' (a derivation proposed by Johnson), as well as the Old French *boudin*. There is the possibility of a link to the Old English *puduc*, meaning a 'swelling', but a clearer derivation would be from the Old French, which appeared in Anglo-Norman as *bodin*, found in Middle English as 'puding' from 1287. English even gave the word back to Latin, as *pudingum*, a Late Latin usage dated to 1245. At this time a pudding was effectively a sausage, and it was not until the seventeenth century that the 'pudding cloth' or 'tammy' brought about boiled or steamed puddings. For a long time these were still a mixture of sweet and savoury (white and black puddings have retained the connection with sausages), so that an eighteenth-century pudding to be eaten with beef might have almonds, cream and sugar, as well as suet and breadcrumbs; the mix of sweet and savoury is retained in the 'plum pudding' (from 1630), or 'Christmas pudding' (from 1858).

**Rarebit**. Traditionally, toasted cheese has always been highly favoured in Wales; there is a sixteenth-century story about unruly Welshmen being lured out of heaven by St Peter crying '*Cause Babe!* (*caws pobi* in modern Welsh), 'that is as moche as to say "Rosty'd chese"'. Neither the origin of 'rabbit' and 'rarebit' as a name for the dish, nor which of them was used first, are known. The traditional explanation is that 'rare bit', meaning 'delicacy', though not found elsewhere, was corrupted into 'rabbit' but was later re-established as the correct form (a similar pattern to 'asparagus'). Against this, Davidson (2006) points out that 'rabbit' appeared in print long before 'rarebit', and Glasse (1747) gave recipes for 'Scotch rabbit', 'Welch rabbit', and two for 'English rabbits', all of them involving toasted cheese, and all long after the idea that cooked cheese was a Welsh speciality. None of this removes the possibility of a corrupted form taking hold, becoming the established form, eventually to be supplanted by the 'correct' form. The first documented uses of 'rarebit' in the *OED* are as 'rare bit' and later 'rare-bit', indicating the process by which this happened. Alternatively, 'Welsh' in the name may give an indication that the name was imposed from outside, mockingly, as if to say 'whatever you ask for in Wales, you'll get toasted cheese.' Or 'Welsh' here may be, for the English, the equivalent of 'poor man's', as in 'Scotch coffee', hot water flavoured with burnt biscuit. Before the advent of overhead grills, a 'rarebit' involved melting the cheese in a pan, pouring it on to hot bread, and scorching it with a salamander (see **grill**).

**Sandwich**. 'A convenient and economical but a rather suspicious order of culinary preparations' was Meg Dods's 1826 appraisal of sandwiches; by then their reputation was already affected by the poor quality of sandwiches made for sale. Though the origin of the word is well known (from the Earl of Sandwich's need for a snack during a twenty-four hour gambling session around 1760), there had been a long history of eating food on, in and with bread. In the fifteenth century the word *sowle* meant 'anything eaten with bread', and *reresopere* was used to translate the Latin *obsonium*, meaning 'food eaten with bread'.

**Sauce**. Appearing in the fourteenth century as *sawse*, 'sauce' derives, through French, from the Latin *salsa*, meaning 'salt'; the current spelling also is documented from the fourteenth century. Ambrose Bierce, in *The Devil's Dictionary* (1911), defined sauce as 'the one infallible sign of civilization and enlightenment'. From the seventeenth century many references to 'saucepans' (the word was first used in the seventeenth century) specifically mention silver saucepans, which probably mostly meant silver-lined pans; these were recommended for preparing medicines and food for invalids, and even for melting sugar when candying flowers.

**Soup**. A medieval text describes *soppe* as 'a broth wherein there is store of sops or sippets'. A *sop* was a piece of bread dipped in liquid, and a *sippet*, or in an earlier form a *suppet*, was a diminutive of this (*sippet* later came to mean a 'fragment of toasted bread'). These were associated with the Old English words *soppian*, meaning 'to dip', and *supan*, 'to drink or sip' (a *sopa* was 'a small drink'). During the Middle English period these became associated with the Old French *soupe* or *sope*, though 'soup' did not appear until the seventeenth century. A 'sop' or 'soppe' was in a late-sixteenth-century recipe the bread on which duck with cabbage was served. Thus 'soup' seems to derive from words meaning 'to drink' and 'the dish in which either bread was put into liquid or liquid was poured on to bread'. In the mid-eighteenth century Glasse spelt the word as 'soop'. The Old English word for 'soup' was *broth*, which could include *geseaw brothu* (vegetable soup), *henne brothe* (chicken soup) or *fæt broth* (rich soup).

**Vindaloo**. 'Vindaloo' has travelled halfway round the world and back again, though, surprisingly, it did not make it into Hobson-Jobson's *Anglo-Indian Dictionary* (1886) and is recorded by the *OED* as first being used in English in 1888. The chillies essential for vindaloo were taken by the Portuguese to Goa, where the spice became part of a dish called *vin d'alho* from *vinho* and *alho*, meaning 'wine' and 'garlic'.

# Desserts

**Blancmange**. The presence of almonds and rice in medieval *blanc manger*, a savoury dish with spices, sugar and chicken, has been held to indicate a Middle Eastern origin; possibly it travelled to western Europe with returning Crusaders. However, when it arrived in England in the fourteenth century its name was French, meaning 'white food'. It remained a savoury dish until the sixteenth century as its name developed – the *Propre New Booke of Cokery* (1545) gives *bleaw manger* as a boiled capon with rye flour and sugar, left to cool until solid enough to be served in slices. When it reappeared as a dessert from France in the eighteenth century its name was borrowed anew with developing spellings – *blamage* (Bailey, 1736), *blanch mange* (Farley, 1783), *blanc mange* (Dods, 1826), and *blamange* (Acton, 1847).

**Custard**. Around 1600 a 'custard' or *crustarde* (adopted from the French *croustade* in the late fourteenth century) ceased to be a kind of open pie with meat or fruit baked in a milk and egg sauce and became the word for the sauce alone. While Ben Jonson early in the seventeenth century described a master cook being able to 'cut fifty-angled custards' (an example of the custom of cutting the crust of a pie into exciting shapes), Samuel Butler's *Hudibras*, written between 1660 and 1680, has the phrase 'Blaspheme custard through the Nose'. Johnson (1755) links 'custard' to the Welsh *cwstard*, stating that it was a food 'much used in city feasts'. The earlier form of the word gives an indication of its nature – a *Crustarde Lumbarde* was a sweet pie.

The 'custard-apple', introduced into Britain in the seventeenth century, was so called from the soft and yellow fruit, which does taste like custard.

**Fool**. Gooseberry fool is, or was, the most common variation of a kind of dessert mixing puréed fruit with cream or custard. The etymology of 'fool' is unclear: John Ayto, in *The Diner's Dictionary* (1993), speculates that it refers to the light and frivolous idea of the recipe. Glasse (1747) gives other recipes for fool, including 'Westminster fool', a sherry trifle without the fruit or jelly.

**Ice cream**. First served in 1671 as a dish of cream served inside an outer dish of ice, called 'cream ice', ice cream retained this name until the mid-nineteenth century, together with 'ice-cream' (the format used in the *OED*), 'iced cream' from 1688, and 'ice cream' from 1744. The first person in Britain recorded as serving ice cream in a wafer cornet was Agnes Marshall in 1888.

**Jelly**. The Middle English *gely*, previously *gelé*, was derived from boiling calves' feet, providing an important ingredient for medieval recipes – *eyroun engele* were 'eggs in jelly'. The spelling with 'g' remained for some time – Johnson in 1755 and 1790 spelt it 'gelly', as did Barclay's *Complete and Universal Dictionary of the English Language* (1812), while Webster in 1828 preferred 'jelly'. The word originally derived from the Latin *gelata*, meaning 'frozen', which also gave rise to 'congeal' and 'gelatine'. 'Jell-o', a proprietary name dating from the 1930s, largely took over in America for the dessert made from sugar, gelatine and flavourings, which in Britain has been called 'jelly' since the eighteenth century. Smith's 1728 recipe for 'riben jelly' calls for the different layers to be coloured with 'cochineal and spinage'.

**Sundae**. The sundae was supposedly invented to get round prohibitions against selling ice cream on a Sunday, or to avoid upsetting sensibilities, but an alternative origin of the 'sundae' proposes that they were for sale only on Sundays, presumably with altered spelling to draw attention to this. 'Sundaes' appeared in the United States in 1897; an earlier version of the name was 'sundi'.

**Syllabub**. According to legend, Charles II sent a milkmaid to squirt milk directly from a cow's udder into a bowl of spiced wine, but 'syllabubs' had been around for several decades before then. The name seems to have been a Tudor exotic invention, and the spelling may have been established by analogy with 'syllable', possibly a bit of folk etymology referring to the Greek root-words meaning 'putting together'. The core idea of putting the milk to the wine either directly from the cow or as close as possible led to interesting simulations – Bailey's 1736 recipe calls for an instrument called a 'wooden-cow'.

**Tart**. The name for a small open pie was adopted in the fifteenth century from French *tarte*, itself possibly an altered form of *torte*, from the Late Latin *torta*, meaning a 'round loaf'. There was possible influence too from the Middle English 'tart' meaning 'sharp-tasting', from Old English *teart*, since tart-tasting fruit could be sweetened for use in a tart.

**Trifle**. The invention of the metal whisk made possible the whipped cream that topped the trifle, or 'whim wham', of the eighteenth century. 'Trifle' or 'triffel' had existed since the late sixteenth century, but as a dish of boiled cream, set with rennet, sweetened and spiced and sometimes flavoured with rose-water.

# Drinks

**Beer, ale**. *Ealu* or *alu* was the Old English word used for 'ale', the drink made from fermented malt; the addition of hops to brewing from the eighth century produced a drink which lasted longer and needed only half the alcohol content of ale ('ale is not so long lasting as Beere is', Markham, 1623). Old English *beor* referred to any alcoholic drink, including drinks fermented from berries and herbs, and cider, for which there was no word in Old English. The use of hops died out, and was reintroduced in the fifteenth century, from which point 'bere' was used to describe ale flavoured by hops.

**Coffee**. Before it arrived in Britain, Francis Bacon described in 1627 a drink called *coffa*, drunk in Turkish 'coffa-houses'; Mulcaster's *Generall Table* (of spellings, 1582) included the unexplained word *caffaie*. The drink had arrived from the Arabian peninsula, coffee plants having been transplanted to Yemen from their native Kaffa, in Ethiopia. Though the drink came to Britain via Italy and France, another name for it, 'the Egypte-drinke', showed that early on people were aware of the plant's origins. The change of the first vowel from 'a' to 'o' appears to be due to influence from the Dutch *koffie*. The Arabic *qahwah* was rendered as 'cahuah' by Johnson in 1755; as well as 'coffee', it also means 'wine'.

**Lemonade**. While Wolley's 'limonado' in *The Queen-like Closet* (1670) was rather alcoholic, current 'lemonade' may mean a clear or cloudy drink made from lemon-juice and sugar, or one made from clear carbonated water with lemon flavouring and sweeteners; this ambiguity is compounded by variations in regional usage. In the United States and Canada 'lemonade' is used for the first form, while 'lemon-lime', 'soda-pop' or proprietary names are used for the second (in various regions or countries, including Chicago, Wales and Canada, the word 'pop' is used for the clear fizzy drink). In Britain, New Zealand and Australia 'lemonade' is used for the clear form, while the drink made from lemons is usually described as 'real lemonade' or 'old-fashioned lemonade'. However, fizzy clear sweet lemonade is occasionally marketed in Britain as 'original lemonade', hopelessly confounding the issue. The '-ade' suffix comes via a number of Romance languages from the Latin -ata, meaning in this case 'resulting from' or 'made from'.

**Tea**. Tea arrived in England in 1658; early recommendations that it be drunk hot with sugar and egg-yolks (1664) were fortunately rejected. Johnson, an obsessive tea-drinker, correctly proposed a Chinese origin; the *Cha jing* is an eighth century classic text on tea by Lu Yu. Tea's journey to English traversed Indonesia, Holland and France, though the Portuguese *cha* was known about in England from 1598. The early pronunciation and spellings *tay* and *tey* reflect the Dutch and French words, but *cha*, *chah* or *char* re-appeared and blossomed in the twentieth century as slang for 'tea'.

**Wine**. The Old English word *win* was acquired by the first Germanic settlers before they arrived in England and is found in the early-eighth-century *Beowulf*. Very few European languages did not acquire some form of the Latin *vinum*, found as far apart as Old Slavic *vino* and Old Irish *fin*. Similar words in Armenian, Greek, Abyssinian, Georgian and Albanian indicate an Indo-European origin.

**Water.** Johnson (1755), clearly having difficulty in defining water, quoted a long account of Newton's definition, describing it as 'a very fluid salt, volatile and void of all savour or taste', while Webster in 1828 offered two paragraphs of meteorology and chemistry, with a brief mention of its necessity to life. Most dictionaries agree that the taste of water is due to additives, and that water itself is 'tasteless' (Collins, 2007).

# Nuts

**Almond**. Almonds arrived in England probably with returning Crusaders (though Johnson, 1755, included a theory that the word came from *Allemand*, 'supposing that almonds came to France from Germany'). They were used extensively in medieval and later recipes; Glasse (1747) even had a recipe for 'almond soup', including the warning 'if you don't be very careful it will curdle'. Partridge (1982) traces the word back through Middle English *almande*, Old French *allemande*, Vulgar Latin *amandula*, Latin *amygdala* (Modern Spanish has *amigdala* for the glands inside the jaw), and Greek *amugdale*, to a possible source in Hebrew *magdi'el*, meaning 'precious gift from God'.

**Cashew**. A native of Brazil, the word 'cashew' came via Portuguese from the Tupi *acajú*, the name of the tree. This may have arrived via French, though in French *acajou* means 'mahogany', which is a totally unrelated tree. Contact with Portuguese would have come in the seventeenth century as cashew trees were transplanted for cultivation first in the East Indies and then in India.

**Coconut**. The three dots on the underside of a coconut resemble a 'grimace', *coco* in Portuguese. Sixteenth-century Portuguese traders in India knew that rather than adopting a local name, *tenga* or *narle*, they were renaming the nut, previously known in Europe as 'Indian nut'; it arrived in England as 'coco' or 'coquo', later being called 'coquo-nut', 'coquernut' and 'cokar'. Johnson (1755) included 'coconut' under the heading 'cocoa', a confusion which was compounded by the corruption of 'cacao' into 'cocoa' around the same time, and which lasted well into the mid-nineteenth century, when the spellings 'cocoa-nut' and 'cokernut' were still in use. 'Cocoanut' lasted into the 1930s.

**Hazelnut**. The eighth-century *hæselnutu* in Britain was widely cultivated from the Anglo-Saxon period, and by medieval times two distinct types of nut were defined: shorter 'cobs' or 'cobnuts', and longer 'filberts'. 'Cobnuts' were originally 'cobill-nuts', related to 'cobble', meaning a 'smooth round stone', while 'filbert' derives from the name St Philibert, whose feast day, 22 August, marks the period when the nuts are ripening.

**Walnut**. The Old English *walhhnutu* reflects the Anglo-Saxons' perception of the nut as 'foreign'– *wal-* being the Old English for 'foreign', seen in the word 'Welsh' (the Welsh being the Celtic peoples pushed across Britain by the Anglo-Saxon settlers from AD 450). However, many contemporary languages described the nut as foreign – it is *walnut* in Middle Low German, *walnote* in Middle Dutch, *walhnot* in Old Norse. C. T. Onions, in *The Oxford Dictionary of English Etymology* (1966), proposes an origin from Low Dutch, between AD 700 and 1100. As walnuts were popular throughout the Roman Empire and have always been popular in France (the French *noix* means both a 'nut' and by default a 'walnut'), it seems reasonable to suppose that the 'foreign place' was France: another Old English recipe calls them *frencisen hnutu*. However, evidence that the Romans brought walnut cultivation to Britain would imply that the nuts were 'foreign' to the Germanic migrants who encountered them when they arrived in England – walnuts were perceived as foreign just as the existing population was. Markham in 1625 spelt them as 'wale-nuts', and the spelling 'wallnut' (Glasse, 1747) developed in the eighteenth century, probably from a mistaken assumption of a connection with walls.

# In the Cupboard

**Chocolate**. Confusion between two Nahuatl (Aztec) words, *xocolatl* and *cacaua-atl*, possibly lies at the root of the confusion between 'chocolate', 'cocoa' and 'cacao'. Early chocolate was made from both cacao seeds and seeds from the *pochotl* tree, roasted, ground and mixed into a paste, which when dry was known as 'nibs', an expression still in use. When it first came into use in England, chocolate was called 'chaculate' but was also spelt 'jocolat' and 'jacolatt'; in 1672 Wolley's recipe included egg-yolks with hot water, sugar and scraped 'chaculate'. 'Cocoa' is made from the ground seeds of the 'cacao'; the word 'cacao' began its transformation to 'cocoa' about 1700, but it was not until around 1800 that 'cocoa' was used to describe the drink.

**Crisps**. Crisps in Britain are dry, cold, thin and brittle slices of potato fried in oil or fat, known in the United States as 'chips' or 'potato chips'. The American term 'Saratoga chips' refers to a story that they were invented in a Saratoga restaurant in 1853 (the *OED* documents it from 1880), but this story is disputed, and it seems likely that crisps/chips developed over a long period.

A tantalising recipe found in medieval cookery books called *Cryspe* or *Cryppys* describes a batter made of egg-white, flour, sugar and honey, fried in lard, though at this time 'crisp' meant 'curly' rather than 'brittle'. By 1706 Evelyn was using 'crisp' to describe fried foods. The arrival of potatoes and, in the eighteenth century, their wider use led to fried potato recipes in Glasse (1747) and the following recipe in Farley (1783): 'Cut your potatoes into thin slices as big as a crown piece and fry them brown.' This would seem to be a fair description of how to make crisps, though the serving suggestion is rather challenging: 'Pour melted butter, sack [sherry] and sugar over them.' Kitchiner's recipe from 1823 is closer: 'As soon as the lard boils … put in the slices (or shavings) of potato, and keep moving them till they are crisp … Lay them to drain; send them up with a very little salt sprinkled over them.' Only the name was missing, first documented by the *OED* from 1929 in Britain.

**Jam**. Webster's 1828 *Dictionary* included both 'jam' and 'jelly' as words for a fruit conserve, but by this time 'jam' was the established word in Britain, the distinction between 'jelly' (clear) and 'jam' (containing fruit pulp) being maintained more strongly in the United States. Fruit jellies (spelt 'gelly', showing the link with 'gelatine') were popular in the Tudor period, but these were desserts rather than conserves. Johnson, like many others since, puzzled over the origin of the word, which first appeared in print in 1706. Smith in 1728 spelt the word 'gam', while Glasse in 1747 spelt it 'giam', possibly to ensure a phonetic transcription, as 'i' and 'j' were both still printed as 'i' at that time. Some association with the verb 'to jam' seems unavoidable, though this is first documented around the same time. Bailey's *Universal Etymological English Dictionary* (1727) does not include the word at all.

**Ketchup**. 'Catchup' and 'catsup' appeared in English towards the end of the seventeenth century, adopted from the Malay *kechap*, which was from the Chinese *koetsiap*, meaning 'seafood sauce'. It is possible that both 'catchup' and 'catsup' were folk-etymology. The form 'ketchup' appeared in the early eighteenth century, and all three were in use in *Chambers's Etymological Dictionary* (1867), but by 1936 only 'ketchup' was in use in Britain. In the United States both 'ketchup' and 'catsup' were used in the 1960s; in the United States 'ketchup' has been lost, while in Canada 'catsup' has largely disappeared.

Eighteenth-century ketchups were made from a variety of ingredients, usually mushrooms and walnuts, though occasionally fish or shellfish were used; there was also a vogue for making 'catchup that will last twenty years'. Kitchiner in 1823 gave a recipe for a highly concentrated version, which he called 'Double cat-sup, or dog-sup'.

**Liquorice**. A fifteenth-century leechbook (book of medicinal recipes) includes 'liquorice' as an ingredient in a treatment for migraine. The root, containing a substance with fifty times the sweetness of sugar, was probably brought to England by returning Crusaders; it was successfully cultivated in the grounds of the Cluniac priory of St John in Pontefract, Yorkshire. The name is an anglicisation of a Greek word meaning 'sweet root', rendered in Latin as *glycyrrhiza*, which entered English around 1200 as *licoriz*, developing through 'licorace' (1670) and 'liquorish' (possibly a folk etymology spelling) to the current spelling; it is spelt 'licorice' in the United States and often in Canada.

**Marmalade**. 'That first necessity of the Englishman's breakfast table', according to Jekyll (1930), marmalade, spelt *marmulate* by Digbie in 1669, has changed considerably since it first arrived in Britain. The Portuguese *marmelada* came from *marmelo*, meaning 'quince', from the Latin *malomellum*. Marmalade was quince conserve from the time it arrived in England, probably with Eleanor of Castile, the wife of Edward I, in 1254. Quinces were enormously expensive – sixteen times the price of apples in the 1290s – and they remained a luxury food: a gift of quince marmalade was used as a royal bribe to get a post at Henry VIII's court. The 1470 *Boke of Nurture* refers to *chare de quynces*, which would have been a French version, *chare* deriving from *carnis*, the Latin for 'meat'; quinces were also called *wardons* or *wardouns* at this time. Markham (1623) specified a 'marmalade of oranges', and the automatic association of 'marmalade' with citrus fruits began only in the eighteenth century. In 1828 Webster still linked it primarily to quinces; only in Scotland, he claimed, was it made with Seville oranges. In the eighteenth century a 'marmalade madam' was slang for a 'prostitute'.

**Marmite**. The Middle French word *marmite*, used from the fourteenth century, meant a 'cooking pot', and such a device has appeared on the labels of jars of Marmite since they were first sold in 1902. As a word for a cooking pot, 'marmite' has been in use since the sixteenth century and is still found occasionally.

**Marzipan**. The usual word for this was 'marchpane' until into the twentieth century. Webster (1828) proposed a derivation from Latin *panis*, meaning 'bread', while Johnson (1755) linked it to the French *massepan* (French rationalised the spelling to *massepain*, giving a misleading link to bread). Early documentation of 'marchpane', according to Colquhoun (2007), dates from the time of the Crusades and does not mention almonds, which became integral to the recipe only in the Tudor period, when there were such delights as 'marchpane tarts' with gold-leaf decoration (*The Treasurie of Commodious Conceites*, John Partridge, 1584); but no other authorities date the word before the sixteenth century.

Several theories have been put forward for the origin of the word: a Burmese port, Martaban, which exported glazed porcelain jars to the Middle East, which were used for storing sweetmeats; the name of a medieval Italian coin, which gave its name to a container, and so its contents; a Yemeni word for a 'seated person', referring to a seated image of Christ on a European coin, later used as a pattern for a cake; Italian words for 'March bread' or 'St Mark's bread'; and the Late Latin *maczapanum*, meaning a 'box for jewellery', which eventually became the Middle French *massepain*, meaning a 'box for confectionery'. A derivation from late-fifteenth-century German *marzipan* and the Italian *marzapane*, both referring to the almond delicacy, seem plausible. The reversal from 'marchpane' to 'marzipan' may have been due to German influence in the mid-nineteenth century. Evelyn in 1706 used 'macaron' to mean 'almonds beaten to a paste' ('makroons' in Wolley, 1675), but before then 'macaroons' was an anglicisation of *macaroni*.

**Mayonnaise**. The story that 'mayonnaise' celebrates the 1756 French capture of the town of Mahon, capital of Minorca, seems unlikely, given that the word first appeared fifty years later. Similarly to be consigned to myth is the story that the sauce was designed by the doctor of Mary, Queen of Scots, who called it *mer en aise* ('comfort at sea'). Other suggestions are that it is a corruption of *bayonnaise*, meaning 'a sauce from Bayonne', or that it derives from the Old French word *moyeu*, meaning 'yolk of an egg'. The first documented spelling in English was 'mayonese', in 1830 (*OED*).

**Pickle**. Preserving foodstuffs in the medieval period was mostly done by smoking or treating with salt; *pekill*, in the late fourteenth century, meant a highly flavoured sauce and probably came from Middle Dutch *pekel*, meaning 'pickle' or 'brine'. In the seventeenth and eighteenth centuries the range of pickled provender included pickled ash-tree seeds, pickled samphire, pickled potato fruits and pickled cowslips. *Pickile lila* appeared in 1694, becoming 'Indian pickle or piccalillo' by 1783.

**Sugar**. Sugar extracted from sugar-cane was being exported to Europe from Persia from the seventh century, though it had been known about in the eastern Mediterranean for many centuries (Alexander the Great sent some home from India). The early Crusaders were entranced by the 'honey-reeds' they found growing around Tripoli and sent home their product, called *zucra*. The word derives ultimately from Sanskrit *sarkara*, meaning 'pebble' or 'grit' (describing the crystals), via the Arabic *sukkar* and the Persian *shakar*, which became the Greek *sakaron* and the Latin *saccharon*. These eventually became the Medieval French *sukere* and *sucre*. The earliest spellings in English, from the thirteenth century, are variations on *sucere* or *zuker*, with *sugure* appearing soon afterwards; the established spelling dates from the sixteenth century.

Around this time sugar was used extravagantly, even in meat dishes, though preparing it for use required clarifying, boiling it in water with egg-white and skimming; Farley (1783) instructs the reader in how to do this 'to five degrees' – boiling it for longer periods till it developed from candy, to blown, to feathered, to crackled and finally to 'carmel' sugar. Producing feathered sugar required the cook to 'shake [the skimmer] over the pan, then give it a sudden flirt behind you, and if it be enough, the sugar will fly off like feathers'.

Associated with sugar are 'treacle', 'syrup' and 'molasses'. 'Treacle' derives from the Old English *theriac*, meaning 'antidote to poison', showing its exclusive medicinal use until the Renaissance; the earlier Greek root-word means 'wild animal'. 'Syrup' derives from the Arabic *sharab* and *shurb*, meaning a 'drink', which became the Medieval Latin *sirupus*, and the Middle English *sirop* and *syrupus*, with variations such as *cyrip* and *siryppe* found together within one recipe in the 1390 *Forme of Cury*. *Shurb* also developed into the antique English drink 'shrub', 'a pretty wine and a cordial' according to Smith in 1728. 'Molasses', earlier spelt 'melasses', derives from the Late Latin *mellaceus*, meaning 'honey-like'.

**Toffee**. The United States, Scotland and some parts of northern England have retained the form 'taffy' for 'toffee' (also called 'tablet' in Scotland), documented from 1817 (*OED*). A transcription of East Anglian speech in 1825 records the sweet as 'toughy', though this may be a folk etymology spelling. The first spelling as 'toffee' is by Dickens in 1828 (*OED*). Partridge (1982) places its origin in the United States, documented by Webster in 1828, with a possible derivation from *taffia*, a Caribbean spirit distilled from sugar-cane juice.

**Vitamin**. The nineteenth-century search for the healthiest foods led to ideas such as the absence of nutrition in vegetables (from J. H. Salisbury, promoter of the 'Salisbury steak' or 'hamburger') and that 'meat contains the nutritive constituents of plants, stored up in concentrated form' (A. W. Hofmann, 1876). Hofmann was writing about the work of Justus von Leibig, who thought he had found the 'essence of meat', which he called 'ozmazome', and which would later be marketed as 'meat extract', or Oxo. The same urge to find the essence of nutrition led to the coining in 1912 by Kazimierz Funk of the word 'vitamine', formed from *vita*, meaning 'life', and *amine*, meaning an 'ammonia-based compound'. Later research showed the chemical analysis to be misleading, and a change in the spelling was proposed: 'Vitamin' would be acceptable 'under the standard scheme of nomenclature … which permits a neutral substance of undefined composition to bear a name ending in "-in".' The same paper, by J. C. Drummond in 1920, proposed the adoption of the names Vitamin A, Vitamin B, etc.

# Herbs and Spices

**Basil**. 'Basil' came from Italian via French, but there is some confusion about its Latin and Greek forms. In Greek it was *basilikon*, meaning 'royal', but its Latin form, *basilisca*, had a connection to the basilisk, a monster whose breath was fatal; it was thought that basil was an antidote to the venom.

**Bay**. Words to describe bay-leaves are not found in Middle English before the fourteenth century; the Old English *begbeam* was used to describe a 'bay tree', though *beg* here may refer to the berries, which for a long time were used for their oil and their sharp taste.

**Cayenne**. It is most likely that cayenne derived from the Brazilian Tupi word, *kyynha*. It may be that as the spice was shipped from the port of Cayenne, the capital of French Guiana, that name was close enough to the Tupi word to oust it. Farley in 1783 spelt it 'chyan', and most of the early English spellings ended '-an' rather than '-en'. The *OED* gives 'cayenne' rather than 'cayenne pepper', 'pepper' being an addition in English which is not applied in French. A rather more disturbing addition was the lead that was used in the nineteenth century to increase the weight, and thus the cost, of the spice.

**Cinnamon**. The first documentation of cinnamon in English is as *sinamome* in about 1430 (*OED*). It arrived via French from the Latin *cinnamom* (which Johnson later gave as *cinnamonium*), as a medicine as much as a culinary spice: Markham (1623) offers it as a treatment for 'griefs in the stomacke', spelling it as both 'cinamo' and 'synamom'. Until the seventeenth century it was spelt with a final 'm' or 'n', though Pepys's diary entry for 1 July 1664 has it as 'cynament'. The origin of the word is probably Malayan, but it has not been traced back further than the Hebrew *qinnamon*.

**Curry**. Curry was adopted into English twice, first at the end of the sixteenth century as 'carriel' from the Portuguese *caril*, adopted from the word *karil*, which appears in both Kannada, a language spoken in Karnataka, a state in south-west India, and according to *Hobson-Jobson* (1886) in Canarese, a Malaysian language. Then in 1747 Glasse gave a recipe for 'currey', probably the spelling used by employees of the East India Company, taken directly from Tamil *kari*. 'Curry' took a long time to register with dictionary writers: it did not appear in Johnson's or Webster's dictionaries, though 'curry-powders' could be purchased in London by 1780.

**Ginger**. This word was adopted twice, first directly from Latin into Old English, and later from Middle French. The first route gave the Old English *gingiber* or *gingifer* from the Late Latin *gingiber*, from the Greek *zingiberis*, which itself has been traced back to the Sanskrit *srngavera*, meaning 'horn-body'. The Latin development into Old French *gimgibre* led to the Middle English *ginger*, though *The Forme of Cury* (1390) has *gyngur*. Ginger is native to the East Indies, and Roman coins have been found as far east as Vietnam, facts that attest to the extraordinary nature of early trade in and demand for spices; as ginger was carried and traded across language zones, this would have involved one language influencing and giving words to the next all along the way.

**Herbs, spices**. Markham wrote in 1623 that the cook 'must know all Hearbs', while Fernandez-Armesto, in *Food, A History* (2001), has shown that the spice trade relates fundamentally to the historical balance of power between East and West. Rather than disguising the taste of old food, spices enhanced fresh food and, being expensive, were socially differentiating. Both words entered English in the thirteenth century: 'spice' derives from the Latin *species*, meaning 'sort', via Old French *espice*, while 'herb' is from Latin *herba*, meaning 'grass or herb', via Old French *erba*. The 'h' in 'herb' was not sounded until the nineteenth century, a usage maintained in the North America.

**Mint**. The Old English *minte*, which became Middle English *mynte*, was a mixture of the Greek *mintha* and the Latin *menta*. It first appeared in Old English texts as a medicinal rather than culinary herb. Greek mythology proposed that Mintha was a nymph whose charms attracted the attention of Hades, the god of the underworld; Hades' wife Proserpine reacted by changing the nymph into a plant.

**Mustard**. The word 'mustard' comes not from the plant itself but from the method of processing it for the table. The Latin *sinapis* developed into the Old English *sinop*, but when ground to a powder it was mixed with vinegar, known as *must*, another Old English word (a fifteenth-century recipe instructs that the ground mustard should be passed through a *farce*, a 'sieve', to sift it). The mixed paste was called *mostard*, after the Old French *moustarde* or *moutarde*. An isolated use of the word *warkecok* for 'mustard', in a fifteenth-century vocabulary, may have been very local.

**Parsley**. The Romans introduced parsley to Britain, but the Latin word *petresilium* arrived in England again five centuries after the legions had left. The development into the Old English *petersilie* was only one of a number of routes and occasions of the word's entering English. Old English also had the word *stanmerce* ('stone' plus *merce* – see **celery**); 'stanmarch' is an old name for 'alexanders' or 'horse-parsley'. The Normans reintroduced the word as *persil* or *percile*, which became the Middle English *parcel*; a single documented spelling of *persilie*, around 1200 (*OED*), may have led to the Middle English *parselee* or *percilye*. Johnson linked it to the Welsh *persli*, which was probably adopted from Middle English rather than vice versa (many Germanic languages adopted a form of *petresilium*, and modern German has retained the same form as Old English). From around the year 1390 there were two versions – *persel* in *The Forme of Cury* (1390), and *persely* in Chaucer's *Cook's Tale* (about 1386). Possibly the dissemination of Chaucer's spelling through Caxton's printed versions fixed that as the established form, as was the case with 'eggs'.

**Pepper**. Supposedly, weight for weight, medieval pepper was worth more than gold, which may at times have been so. In the fifth century barbarians besieging Rome demanded 3,000 pounds of pepper as part of the city's ransom, and the Anglo-Saxon historian Bede left his little store of *piporcornes* to his fellow monks as a bequest. A commodity so desirable would have been a strong incentive to traders to keep routes open, and the spice route from China was firmly established by the second century. The Old English verb *piporian*, meaning 'to pepper', and the existence of Anglo-Saxon recipes for omelettes with sage and pepper, indicate the spice was well-known and used. Before the period of migration to England Germanic languages had acquired the Latin *piper*, itself either a development from the Greek *peperi*, or, like the Greek, an acquisition from India via Persia, coming from the Sanskrit *pippali*.

The 'sweet pepper', or 'capsicum' in the United States, became generally popular in the twentieth century, but the 'hot pepper' or 'chilli', offering an alternative to the peppercorn, quickly spread throughout Europe after it was brought back by Columbus in 1492. A fifteenth-century leechbook (list of medicines) refers to a *longe pep* (long pepper), while Evelyn (1709) described it as 'ginny pepper' (Guinea pepper).

**Sage**. Nathan Bailey said of sage that it was 'endued with so many and wonderful properties, as that the constant use of it is said to be so salutiferous to mankind, as to render them almost immortal'. Sage, being a native of Italy, was probably a Roman introduction, though its name probably arrived via post-1066 clerical journeys. In Ælfric's *Colloquy* (about 1000) it appears as *fenfearn*. The Latin *salvus*, meaning 'safe', gave rise to the plant's name *salvia*, referring to its medicinal properties. In Middle French this appeared as *sauge*, which became the Middle English *sawge* and *sage*.

**Salt**. Old English had *sealt* and *salt* for 'salt', with *salgeme* in Middle English meaning 'rock-salt'. Johnson (1755) traced it back to Gothic *salt* and Latin *sal*. There are so many similar words in European languages, from Cornish *sal* to Old Bulgarian *salyi*, that an Indo-European root-word '*sal-*' is widely accepted.

# Cooking

**Bain-marie**. The Latin *balneum mariæ* is documented from fourteenth-century France; the name possibly derives from the association of the mother of Jesus with gentleness. Until the nineteenth century the Latin form was used – Bailey (1736) uses 'Balneum mariæ or Vaporis' and 'balneo mariæ or Bath Mary'. The use of this method by the great French chef Carême, who cooked for the Prince Regent for two years from 1816, was instrumental in fixing it as 'bain-marie', though Kitchiner in 1823 felt it was necessary to explain and translate it, as 'water-bath'. In *Practical Sanitary and Economic Cooking* (1890), Mary Abel tried to introduce the term 'steamer' from Europe to the United States, but 'double-boiler' has remained the established term; 'bain-marie' is rarely used in North America.

**Boil**. The Old English *seothan* developed into the Middle English 'seethe', meaning 'to boil in water', found as frequently as 'to boil' in seventeenth-century recipes, and still used in this way in 1936, according to Wyld (1936). 'To boil' derives from Old French *boillir*, and ultimately from the Latin *bulla*, meaning 'bubble'.

**Cauldron**. In medieval England a 'cauldron' (also spelt 'caldron') allowed several kinds of simultaneous cooking – broths, puddings boiled in cloth, and entire meals in a bain-marie. The Anglo-Norman *caudron*, which developed from the Latin *calidaria*, meaning 'cooking pot', and *caldus*, meaning 'hot', became the Middle English *caudroun* and *cawdron*. It is possible that the intrusive 'l' appeared later as a result of writers being influenced by the Latin *caldus*.

**Chef**. In seventeenth-century France professional cooks were elevated to the rank of *chevalier*. However, the title *chef de cuisine* was first used by a later great French cook, Carême. The first documented use of the word 'chef' in English to describe the head cook of a kitchen was in 1842 (*OED*).

**Cooker, stove**. The famous Reform Club chef Alexis Soyer, a great pioneer of gas as a cooking fuel, in the 1840s designed one of the first domestic gas cookers, called the 'Phidomageireion', from the Greek words meaning 'thrifty kitchen'; perhaps fortunately, he failed to patent it. Though gas stoves were displayed at  the Great Exhibition in London in 1851, the word 'cooker' was not used until 1884 (*OED*). Until then the word usually applied was 'stove', deriving from a Germanic word for a 'steam bath'; the word and meaning were adopted twice, in the Old English period as *stofa*, and in the fifteenth century as *stofe* or 'stove'. Only in the sixteenth century was the word used for a cooking-stove. A 'range', originally a 'range stove', dates from around 1800.

**Grill, broil**. Grilling in the modern (British) sense, requiring an overhead heat source, was, before the advent of gas or electric grills, done with a heated metal disc called a salamander. Occasionally recipes recommended using a fire shovel (Bailey in 1736 proposed using one to 'ice' – presumably 'melt' – the sugar on the top of an omelette); but a well-appointed kitchen would have had a salamander – Agnes Jekyll two hundred years later used hers for browning the tops of oysters. In the twelfth century the Anglo-Norman term *gridilie* was used for a small gridiron, and this eventually became *grille*, documented in English in the seventeenth century as 'grill', though Markham (1623) still referred to a 'gridyron'. Cooking in front of a fire was 'broiling', for Dods 'the most delicate manual office of the cook' (1826); the term began to disappear in British English in the nineteenth century. Broiling might be done in a 'Dutch oven', dating from the eighteenth century – basically a vertical spit set within a curved metal plate to reflect the heat. The spit might be turned mechanically by a bottle-jack, a spring providing a slow rotation for the meat. 'Broil' can be traced through Old French *bruiler*, meaning 'to burn', to the Vulgar Latin *per-ustulare*, meaning 'to burn totally'. 'Broil' has been retained in the United States for grilling using a heat source overhead or underneath.

**Hob**. It would be nice to think that 'hob' was related to 'hobgoblin', and there may be a tenuous connection. The 'hob' of a grate or a kitchen range was a warming plate at the top, formerly a 'hub'. Partridge (1982) proposes that for a 'hub', both in this case and in the centre of a wheel, there is an essential concept of something sticking up or out from its surroundings (as in 'hobnail'), and that it may be a kind of nickname for a familiar object, like the word 'jack'; 'hob' was formerly a diminutive for the name Robin, and this is how it is used in 'hobgoblin'. The first use of 'hob' for a cooking plate on a cooker was in 1962 (*OED*).

**Kettle**. 'Kettle' developed from the Latin *cucuma* and *catillus*, through Old Norse *ketill*, Old English *cetel* or *cytel*, to the Middle English *ketil*. All these words retain something of the sound of water boiling in a metal container, an idea that appealed to the seventh-century etymologist Isidore of Seville. But the term has been used for vessels for purposes other than boiling water – Sorbière (1698) referred to 'little tin-kettles ... with small-coals kindled, to light ... pipes withal'. The problem is knowing what shape of container the word actually applies to. Kenelm Digbie (1669) cooked a lamprey in 'a kettle with a narrow mouth'; for Johnson in 1755, 'the name of pot is given to the boiler that grows narrower towards the top, and of kettle to that which grows wider', while for Webster in 1828 it was 'a vessel ... with a wide mouth, usually without a cover'. The *OED* cites a text from 1866 describing a kettle whistling, which would seem to indicate a spout. For Farley, in London in

1783, veal could be stewed in a 'kettle', and Kitchiner, forty years later, refers to a 'soup kettle', presumably with a wide top. Mrs Beeton (1861) refers to several types of kettle: a 'tea-kettle', a 'gravy-kettle', a 'fish-kettle' (oval in shape), and a 'glaze-kettle' (a double-boiler for keeping glazes liquid). *Delineator* recipes from the United States in the 1920s and 1930s show kitchens with and without spouted kettles, while kettles, where documented, could be both 'a deep fat frying kettle with basket' (1930) or a 'tea-kettle' placed on the table ready for a very English 'afternoon tea' (1931). Possibly the spouted kettle travelled from Britain only to those parts of the English-speaking world where regular tea-drinking was adopted or imported, Canada, Australia and New Zealand particularly, while the general use of the word for a 'boiling pot' was continued anywhere outside Britain.

**Oven**. The idea of an enclosed cooking space probably developed from the earliest cooking done in a cooking pit. This is mirrored by one theory for the development of words leading to 'oven', proposed in *Chambers's Etymological Dictionary* (1867): Sanskrit *agni*, meaning 'fire', leading to Latin *ignis*, was connected to the Gothic *auhns*, which led to the Icelandic *ofn* and Old English and German *ofen*. The Old English *ofen* led to the specific word *hlafofen*, meaning 'bread oven', reflecting the use of ovens primarily to bake bread or pies, meat usually being spit-roasted or broiled. As controls of temperature developed in eighteenth-century ovens, ovens were described as 'quick' or 'slow', rather than 'high' or 'low', a terminology still in use.

**Poach**. The original idea of poaching eggs seems to have been that the plunging of an egg's contents into boiling water causes the white to solidify from the outside, creating a 'pocket' for the yolk. The Middle English form *pocche* derived from the Middle French *pocher*, from *poche*, meaning 'bag' – a fifteenth-century cookbook has a recipe for 'eyroun en poche'. All other poached dishes, fish, fruit, meat, etc, cooked in simmering liquid derive from this.

**Roast**. The Old English word *braed* meant 'broad', thus *braedan* meant 'spread in front of a fire' or 'roast'. In the thirteenth century *roste* or *rosti* appeared in English, from the Old French *rostir*, though from a Germanic rather than Latin source; 'roasting' meant specifically cooking before an open fire rather than in an oven, as can be seen in the definition in *Chambers's Etymological Dictionary* (1867), 'to cook before fire'.

**Simmer**. This was originally to *simper* and changed to 'simmer' about the middle of the seventeenth century. It is generally agreed that, like 'kettle', the origin of the word lies in the sound, echoing the gentle bubbling of hot liquid cooking. However Skeat (1882) pointed out the possibility of a Germanic root *sim*, seen in words for to 'buzz' or 'hum' in German, Danish and Swedish.

**Stew**. 'Stove' and 'stew' came from the same source – 'stews' were originally vessels for boiling water, and later rooms heated in this way for steam baths. From this the word developed in the fourteenth century to take on the meaning of a public bath, and from that to a brothel, no doubt because of the easy soliciting that went on at public baths.

**Toast**. 'To toast' was adopted from Old French *toster* in the fourteenth century; many recipes or descriptions emphasised that the bread for toasting (to make 'tostes') should be high-quality. This is seen in Digbie's and Wolley's seventeenth-century recipes, using 'manchet', and Moritz's 1782 complaint against most bread and butter – 'thin as poppy leaves' – except for 'another kind of bread … incomparably good. This is called toast.'

**Wash up**. The specific use of 'wash up' as to 'wash the dishes after a meal' is documented by the *OED* (online) from 1751. Strangely, the *OED* does not offer a separate entry for to 'dry up' in the sense of 'drying wet dishes after washing up', but includes an example of this usage dating from 1932.

# Meals and Places

**Banquet**. Coming from French and Italian words meaning 'little table', 'banquet' has meant different things at various times. Though from the fifteenth century it was occasionally used for the great feasts that were displays of wealth used to confirm political allegiance, these were more often described using the older word 'feast', from the Latin *festa*. From the sixteenth century a 'banquet' was more often a light meal where fruit wines and sweetmeats were served, or a display of culinary ingenuity in making statuesque desserts, such as the sugar castles, mermaids and unicorns made in 1591 to entertain Elizabeth I. Markham (1623) offered recipes for 'banquetting stuffe and conceited dishes' (quince jelly, hippocras and cakes). By 1755 a 'banquet' had become, in Johnson's words, simply a 'feast'.

**Breakfast**. Around 1780, 'for some while it had been customary to defer the first meal of the day till 10 o'clock,' wrote Palmer (1952). Considering that daylight largely governed working hours, a summer breakfast some five hours after waking would have meant that waiting to 'break your fast' would have been an ordeal. However, Webster's second definition, 'a meal, or food in general', reminds us that the word does not limit eaters to any time of the day – hence the phrase 'wedding breakfast'. 'Breakfast' replaced the seventeenth-century 'jenticulation', an anglicisation of the Latin *jentaculum*. See **dinner**.

**Chow**. Seldom used in Britain, the word 'chow' in the United States is often supposed to derive from the story that poor Chinese immigrants in the nineteenth century ate dog-meat, which is folk etymology at best. A more likely source is the Cantonese word *chaau*, meaning 'to fry or cook', which would have been a Chinese component of the pidgin developed in the course of trade between China and English-speaking countries; alternatively it is a Tagal dish from Manila called *chau-chau* (Hobson-Jobson).

**Dining-room**. About 1600 the 'dining-room' began to take the place of the 'hall' for meals, though it was to remain a new-fangled word for 150 years. By the tenth edition of Johnson's *Dictionary*, in 1790, the dining-room was 'the principal apartment in the house'; the introduction of service *à la Russe*, in the early nineteenth century, allowed hosts to use the dining-room as a stage on which to display their wealth and their ability to manage a meal as an event, with waiters serving guests individually. In the nineteenth century the term 'dining-rooms' was extended to mean 'restaurant'.

**Dinner**. For a period of five hundred years until the sixteenth century 'dinner', from the French *disner*, was the first and main meal of the day. A fifteenth-century *nominale* (vocabulary of nouns) translates the Latin *jantaculum* (later used in English as *ienticulum*) as *dynere*; the Latin word actually means 'breakfast'. The structure of the word is the negative prefix *dis-* attached to the word *ieiunium*, meaning 'hunger or not eating', and appears in Spanish as *desayunar* and in French as *dejeuner*. 'Dinner' gradually moved from early morning in the medieval period to mid-morning in the sixteenth century, but by the fifteenth century there had evolved a meal between dinner and supper called the *myd-dyner under-mete*, a phrase whose second part was Old English for an 'afternoon dinner'.

**Fast food**. Fast food has been around for as long as people have been living in cities, though the term 'fast food' is dated only from 1951 (*OED*). Fernández-Armesto (2001) offers key dates and ideas such as Piers Plowman in the fourteenth century hearing the London street vendors cry 'Hot pies, hot!'; the first drive-in restaurant in 1937; and from 1948 the elimination of cutlery at one fast-food outlet. To these may be added the London 'chop-house' from around 1700, and the 'shilling ordinary', a cheap restaurant, from around 1800. But ways of speeding up the production of food appear in recipe books from the eighteenth century; 150 years before Oxo, Hannah Glasse offered a recipe for 'pocket soop', soup prepared and reduced to 'a dry hard piece of glew', for later reconstitution.

**Grub**. Partridge (1974) documents 'grub' as a slang word for food from 1659; though the word had been in use for about 150 years for the larva of an insect, it is not clear whether the idea of food comes from this. The word developed from Old English words for 'to dig' and is related to 'grave'.

**Lunch**. For Johnson, 'lunch' and 'luncheon' meant as much food as one's hand could hold, probably coming from 'clunch' or 'clutch'. In terms of textual documentation, 'luncheon' predates 'lunch' by a few years, both appearing at the end of the sixteenth century. Weekley (1912) believed that 'luncheon', meaning a 'piece or hunk of bread', was a development of 'lunch', by analogy with 'nuncheon', which it replaced. In Old English, a drink taken at midday was a *noon scenc* (pronounced 'shench'); by the mid-fourteenth century this had developed into a *nonschenche*, an 'early afternoon drink break'. By the time of Johnson's *Dictionary* (1755) 'nunchin' was 'a piece of victuals eaten between meals', and there are records of 'nunching' in the Midlands and 'nuncheon' in Wiltshire in the 1950s. In 1829 there was a demarcation of snobbery between 'lunch' and 'luncheon', 'lunch' being proposed by the Almack's Club as the proper term. But fashion in words is constantly mutable: in 1927 the *Delineator* magazine offered a menu for a 'luncheon' for a 'Bride's Recipe Shower', and in 1930 Jekyll offered a menu for 'a winter shooting-party luncheon'. For the *Collins English Dictionary* (2007), 'luncheon' is now mainly used for a formal lunch, except for the mixture of cereal and cooked pork called 'luncheon meat', a curious survivor from the days of Second World War rationing.

**Picnic**. According to the *New English Dictionary* (1909), a picnic was 'a fashionable social entertainment in which each person present contributed a share of the provisions'; in the United States this kind of meal has become a 'potluck', which in Britain developed the sense of a meal with one or more guests for which nothing special has been prepared. 'Picnic' was adopted from the French seventeenth-century *pique-nique*, meaning 'to pick a little amount'; the specific association with eating out of doors probably originated in England in the early nineteenth century and then moved back across the Channel.

**Restaurant**. In eighteenth-century France, only licensed cookshops and inns could serve solid food, to be eaten on the premises, until in 1765 a Parisian street-soup-vendor named Boulanger, who described his soups as *restaurant* ('restorative') widened his menu to include 'ragouts' (then a dish of meat in spicy sauce). This fell foul of regulations, so he devised a dish of sheep's feet in white sauce. The licensed food-sellers prosecuted him, but lost; the ensuing fame of both cook and dish led others to follow his lead using the name *restaurant*, which was retained when the sellers were able to work from settled premises. In fact it seems more likely that the monopoly of licensed food premises was broken in 1766 by the inventor Mathurin Roze de Chantoiseau, who sold from his own premises a broth designed to 'restore' his customers. The word first appeared in English in the early nineteenth century.

**Snack**. Pepys's diary entry for 5 January 1667 mentions 'a snap of victuals' between meals. A 'snack' and a 'snap' were synonymous, 'snap' being probably the older form; both come from the Dutch *snacken*, meaning to 'bite', and, while both have survived, 'snap' is now found as a regional and dialect word, while 'snack' has become the standard form. The *Survey of English Dialects* made in the 1950s found that in the Midlands and South of England a mid-morning snack was called 'elevenses', while in the North of England it was more likely to be called 'tenoclocks' or 'tenses'.

**Supper**. For Johnson 'supper' derived from the French *souper*, meaning 'to eat the evening meal', while for *Chambers's Etymological Dictionary* (1867) it was a direct development from the Old English *supan*, meaning 'to eat the evening meal', and is linked with the verb 'to sup', meaning 'to drink'. The confusion comes from two roots for 'to sup', one being the Old English *supan*, which meant 'to drink', and widened to include 'to take in', and the other being the Old and Middle French *souper*, meaning 'to eat the evening meal'.

# Bibliography

The data on historical cookery books, books on etymology and dictionaries is given where they appear in the text.

Barnhart, R. K. (editor). *Chambers Dictionary of Etymology*. Chambers, 1988.

Baugh, A. C., and Cable, T. *A History of the English Language*. Routledge & Kegan Paul, 2002.

Crystal, D. *The Cambridge Encyclopaedia of the English Language*. Cambridge University Press, 2002.

Davidson, A. *The Oxford Companion to Food*. Oxford, 2006.

Hagen, A. *Anglo-Saxon Food and Drink*. Anglo-Saxon Books, 2006.

*Oxford English Dictionary, Compact Edition*. London, 1979, and online.

Sheard, J. A. *The Words We Use*. Andre Deutsch, 1970.

# Index

# INDEX